a few words
about words

a few words about words

a common-sense look at writing and grammar

Joe Diorio

BEAUFORT
BOOKS

A FEW WORDS ABOUT WORDS

Paperback: 9780825309472
Ebook: 9780825308512

For inquiries about volume orders, please contact:
Beaufort Books
27 West 20th Street, Suite 1102
New York, NY 10011
sales@beaufortbooks.com

Published in the United States by Beaufort Books www.beaufortbooks.com
Distributed by Midpoint Trade Books, a division of Independent Book Publishers
www.midpointtrade.com
www.ipgbook.com

Book design by Mark Karis

Printed in The United States

For Susan, for always believing in me.

Contents

introduction

I HAVE WRITTEN ALL MY LIFE. As a kid, I would write and illustrate my own graphic novels, reaching into the depths of my attention deficit/hyperactivity disorder (ADHD) riddled imagination to make up original stories about a team of superheroes I called the "I.S. Men," or "Intercrime Stoppers." The word "intercrime" was a term that stuck in my brain while watching reruns of the old British television show *The Avengers*. I liked it because it sounded extra evil. My superheroes were Muscle Man, Rubber Man (His limbs could stretch. Get your mind out of the gutter, people.), Molecule Man, and others. All I needed was to read one issue of DC Comics' "Justice League" and my imagination had enough fuel to create an adolescent's canon of stories. How I wish I hadn't stored them in the garbage can in my room, where my Mom quite logically threw them away.

In high school I worked for free as a stringer (basically a freelance journalist) for a local weekly community newspaper covering high school sports and general goings-on at my school. In college, I was a reporter and columnist for the campus newspaper, and for my first three years out of college I worked for daily newspapers in Connecticut. Later, I worked as a public relations professional, corporate speech writer, and later still, I was self-employed as a freelance writer. I even ghostwrote a book for IBM called *The Customer-Centered Enterprise*; don't look for it. It's out of print.

But there is a "but" to all of this; I absolutely stink at English grammar. I always have.

I know, I know. Here's the elephant-in-the-room question: How do I manage to work at jobs that require writing, yet I'm horrible at grammar? I'll answer that question with one of my own: What do you do if you come upon a pothole in the road while driving? You drive around it, right? I do the same thing with writing. I "write around" the problems. Earlier in life, some of those drive arounds were more like Hail Mary passes.

I'm a master at writing around a grammatical problem. Do I need to say someone looked at the ceiling? Rather than tying myself in knots over the "i before e" rule in order to spell ceiling correctly, I'd just write, "He looked above." Is something effective or affective? "It really works," I'd write. Form the plural possessive of a noun? Don't.

To paraphrase Yogi Berra, you can write a lot by avoiding the problems.

But not all grammatical potholes can be avoided, and I make more than my share of mistakes. After 30-plus years as a writer, I still constantly make grammatical mistakes. Right now, I had to double-check myself on the spelling of the word "grammar." (Who among you caught the fact that I unnecessarily used a semicolon a few paragraphs earlier? Gotcha, didn't I?) Know that feature in Microsoft Word where a squiggly red line appears under a misspelled word? The first draft of anything I write looks like a traffic light convention.

Almost every day of my career, my slippery grasp of grammar drove my editors, co-workers, supervisors, and probably more than a few of my readers to the brink of insanity. (I think a few took the leap off insanity ridge rather than keep trying to straighten out my fractured syntax.) The city editor at a newspaper I worked for once threatened the safety of my job—I think the threat of some physical harm may have been thrown in too, just for good measure—if I kept making mistakes.

Once, while dreaming aloud about career aspirations, I said to a co-worker at the newspaper I was working for—a co-worker who knew how bad I was at grammar—that I would someday like to be a newspaper copy editor. He fell into uncontrollable fits of laughter upon hearing that. I guess it's nice to know that my career goals can bring such joy to others.

I can trace my meager knowledge of grammar back to my childhood. Yes, I am about to blame my parents. Sue me. My family moved a lot when I was in elementary school. We didn't know we were house flippers because the term was not in vogue back then, but that's what we were. My dad would buy a house, then we would live in it while he fixed it up (only on weekends, since he had a full-time job at a defense contractor factory). By the time the house was fixed up or improved sufficiently, he and Mom would sell the house, and we would move on to the next house, hopefully making a modest profit along the way.

Moving a lot means I changed schools a lot. And the kids in my new school always seemed to be *ahead* of where I was academically. Or at the very least, they were definitely not on the same page I was on. An undiagnosed case of ADHD did not help me, either. But I digress. (And, by the way, I digress *a lot* in these pages. Apologies in advance if that makes you nuts. You should try talking to me in person.)

Being the one kid in class who wasn't at the same academic benchmark as the other students—or at least that is what it felt like to me—meant I would be embarrassed when called upon by the teacher to answer a question. I would invariably get the answer wrong and had to endure the laughter and taunts from classmates.

By the way, calling them "mates" is suggestive that the other kids in class were friendly toward me. Trust me, these kids were far from friendly. Most reveled in laughing at anyone who seemed slower than them. At least it feels that way when you are on the receiving end of the laughter.

I coped with this situation by doing what any under-achieving kid would do in school in the 1960s. I hid from the teacher's watchful eye. This was probably the start of my navigating around grammatical problems. I made sure to sit behind the kids who were called on a lot. I would raise my hand only *after* the teacher called on someone else. Not so eager as to make the teacher think, "OK, I'll call on Joseph next time," but just enough to make them think I knew the answer. Then, as a deflection move, I *would not* raise my hand when the teacher asked the next question. This cat and mouse game made it look like I was participating. Just like I would write around grammatical problems, I could navigate the "Joseph needs to participate in class" maze by playing my teachers to make them

4

think I was participating yet was never called upon.

This tactic almost worked. Unfortunately, around the time I was in the fourth grade, a teacher told my parents during a conference that she thought I was bored, and therefore, would assign more homework to me in order to keep me engaged. Damn these dedicated public servants. To paraphrase Yoda from *Star Wars*, screwed, I was.

In high school, one teacher discovered my grammatical liability and helped me. Realizing I was hopelessly lost in the grammatical woods, he tutored me after class using the nonsense words method of helping one understand the basics of English grammar. That tactic helped—a little. I could easily identify subject/verb/adjective/noun in the sentence, "The ravenous students quickly devoured a massive pizza," just as long as the sentence I was dissecting comprised nonsense words, such as "The milchy mulchers twongly gribbled a hodday snib." OK, I was getting close. But close doesn't count in grammar, only horseshoes or (so goes the joke) hand grenades.

By the time I was finishing college, I still possessed a Titanic vs. iceberg level of grammatical prowess. In case you are wondering, I am the Titanic in that analogy. With a meager grasp on English grammar, I blindly chose a career path that would have me writing all the time. I became a newspaper reporter.

This was not a surprising career path for me. I was the kid who expressed himself by writing about the adventures of a bunch of imaginary superheroes, so I could write about real heroes by covering the local police and fire departments. (Yes, I really thought that about local journalism. Stop laughing.) Besides, someone once described working as a news reporter as, "Monday is always different from Tuesday, and once in a while, you catch the bad guy." Maybe that's why I liked writing comic books about superheroes. I could create my own story and get the bad guy.

As a newspaper stringer, I had fun writing about the goings-on in my community, even if I was largely assigned to write about my high school football team and their perpetual losing streak. (Did you know a final score in a high school football game can be 79—0? Now you do.) Nevertheless, becoming a newspaper reporter made sense. Amazingly, my college courses focused more on reporting, the business of newspapers and magazines, and less on the actual craft of writing. In this academic phantom zone, I was again skating by with subpar grammatical skills because, well, no one in college bothered to look closely at my writing ... if at all.

Eventually, everyone gets a break. Mine came when an older classmate, who was fascinated with the intricacies of our language—he once wrote a feature based on the fact that a local store displayed a sign that read, "Going out FOR Business." The "for" rather than "of" angle of his story comprised 700 words in newsprint—gifted me a copy of *The Careful Writer* by Theodore M. Bernstein.[1] Reading Bernstein's tongue-in-cheek discussions of grammar slowly helped me improve. The book's 487 pages of granular explanation about words and how they are used—explanations not preceded by "Damn it, Joe" or followed by, "Got it, lunkhead?"—fueled my fascination with language. The word "occupied" always takes the preposition "by" or "with" and, wait, there is a difference between "sometime" and "some time"? There was a level of detail that held me intellectually hostage from the get-go. I started to understand that I could avoid all the grammatical pitfalls I had endured by just *looking stuff up*.

(Quick sidebar: My friend signed the book, "Don't never make none mistakes in your grammar after you read this here book!" I'm going to believe he was being sarcastic in a very friendly way. That's my story. And I'm sticking to it.)

Today, any grammatical skill I have is from long hours and lots of hard work. That does not mean I am a walking grammar reference book. If someone on the fly asks me a grammatical question, I probably won't know the answer off the top of my head. This inevitably prompts the "I thought you knew this stuff" comment. But that's why there is a stack of reference books on my desk. They are not just for show. *I use them.*

Here's my grammatical prowess summed up in an anecdote. One time I was at a meeting of Nashville's chapter of the International Association of Business Communicators to hear a presentation about common mistakes people make when writing. The talented speaker would occasionally toss a grammatical question to the audience, just to keep them engaged. (I suspect he knew my fourth-grade teacher.) A colleague seated to my left kept answering faster than I could. I felt like I was on "Jeopardy" competing against the IBM Watson supercomputer. But this memory drives home the point that you don't have to know the answers off the top of your head, and there is no shame in looking up the answers. When someone once asked Albert Einstein for his telephone number, so goes the story, Einstein looked it up in the phone book. "Why remember something that you can just look up?" he reportedly said. Similarly, I do not memorize whether "also" should follow or precede the verb when I can just as easily look it up. I feel you, Al.

OUR ONGOING FASCINATION WITH LANGUAGE

Our society finds different proverbial shiny objects to hold the collective fascination in many places. In the early days of the United States our group fascination was politics. In her book, *Team of Rivals: The Political Genius of Abraham Lincoln*, Doris Kearns Goodwin explains how politics was a national pastime in America in the mid-1800s.

> "In the only country founded on the principle that men should and could govern themselves, where self-government dominated every level of human association from the smallest village to the nation's capital, it was natural that politics should be a consuming, almost universal concern," she writes.
>
> She continues, "[Over] here, the people of one neighborhood have gathered to learn if a church ought to be built; [over] there, they are working on the choice of representative; farther on, the deputies of a district are going to town in all haste [to] decide about some local improvements. For many ambitious young men in the nineteenth century, politics proved the chosen arena for advancement."[2]

With politics being so popular, it is no surprise that the Lincoln/Douglas debates leading up to the U.S. Senate campaign of 1858 held the population spellbound. Here was the national pastime at its best. And we ate it up to the point where the debates are rightfully chronicled in history books.

Ninety years later, as the cinema held sway, Americans became fixated on organized crime. Hollywood of the 1930s glamorized mob culture with stars like Edward G. Robinson and James Cagney stealing, scheming, and killing their way to the top of their criminal heap. Those dirty rats could hold an audience spellbound.

At around that same time, outside of the movie theaters, the game of baseball was taking hold of the American psyche. "Whoever wants to know the heart and mind of America had better learn baseball, the rules and realities of the game—and do it by watching first some high school or small-town teams," wrote French-born American philosopher Jaques Barzun in 1954.[3] Long before Barzun penned that famous quote, and long before Red Barber was broadcasting baseball games over radio airwaves, any town square on any given summer afternoon would teem with people who followed the pitch-by-pitch reports of their favorite local nine, often delivered to them via telegraph.

Our fascinations are indeed as varied as society itself. Today we can say anything from the latest Tik Tok video while the Kardashians and, perhaps, a political Twitter storm keeps our attention.

Despite these ever-changing trends, the one thread they all have in common—the perpetual shiny object, if you will—is writing. Someone wrote about politics. Someone wrote about baseball. (I won't even try to count how many books, from *The Boys of Summer* to *Bang the Drum Slowly*, have been written.) Someone *wrote all those movie scripts.* Our fascinations are rooted in the written word.

Our love of language goes back even further into history and has seemingly never waned. How we express ourselves has been the subject of fascination ever since the first wall etchings were made in some remote cave.

Said wall etchings were lampooned as graffiti on the wall of a Roman empire-controlled town square in the Monty Python comedy, *Life of Brian,* which shows John Cleese's Roman Centurion using his authoritarian position to correct Graham Chapman as Chapman's character, Brian, was painting anti-Roman Latin graffiti on a wall.

"What's this, then? 'Romanes Eunt Domus?' People called Romanes, they go the house?" Cleese says.

"No, it says 'Romans, go home,'" Chapman replies as he quivers at the realization that he has been caught in the midst of a dirty deed.

"No, it doesn't," Cleese shouts. "What's Latin for 'Roman'? Come on!"

"Romanus," Chapman says.

"[And] the vocative plural of 'annus' is?" Cleese presses.

"Anni," says a cowering Chapman.

"[Correct] Romani."[4]

OK, so based on what we know of history, a centurion probably wouldn't have delivered a lecture on Latin grammar—more likely he would have done what Cleese threatens at the end of the comedic bit (cutting Chapman's jewels off)—but you get the idea. No matter the setting, we constantly discuss, debate, and argue about language. In fact, everyone looks upon American English and discusses and/or criticizes it. Scholars endlessly study ancient manuscripts to determine their precise meaning. For example, most literary scholars agree that the very first word of *Beowulf,* according to most translations from ancient English, is "Listen!" and it suggests that the story was first spoken, not written, and was possibly told around a campfire … without a flashlight to the face, no doubt.[5]

We debate our language, sometimes forever. More than 50 years after he set foot on the moon, we are still questioning whether Neil Armstrong said, "That's one small step for man," or "That's one small step for *a* man." (To the day he died, Armstrong insisted he said the latter, but we all know he said the former. I recall watching the moon landing on a tiny black and white television and asking myself, "Why did Armstrong say it *that* way?")[6]

We evolve our language to fit the physical expression. I find it fascinating that, over time, our language moved from symbols often carved or painted on walls to words, first handwritten then printed; we are slowly moving toward common abbreviations, a hybrid of symbols. Linguist Gretchen McCulloch in *Because Internet: Understanding the New Rules of Language*, discusses the regional preferences for abbreviations. She says "ikr" (I know, right?) is popular in Detroit, while "suttin" (something) is popular in New York. "Af" (as fuck) traces its origin to Los Angeles and eventually began appearing in headlines for the online news source, *BuzzFeed*, signaling some degree of acceptance.[7]

We understand that language, with just the right leverage, can instill leadership, give hope, and provide direction. Actor Michael Gambon, who plays King George V in the movie, *The King's Speech*, laments having to deliver a speech via radio. "In the past, all a King had to do was look respectable in uniform and not fall off his horse. Now we must invade people's homes and ingratiate ourselves with them ... we've become actors!"[8]

A former actor leading a nation may have been viewed as lamentable in the 1930s, but by 1986, someone who once was an actor, President Ronald Reagan, understood the power of the written and spoken word. Reagan addressed the nation on that horrible day in 1986 when the space shuttle, Challenger, exploded shortly after liftoff, killing all seven astronauts on board. The event left an indelible mark on society. Reagan captured the nation's angst when he uttered these words, written by his speechwriter Peggy Noonan,

> "The crew of the space shuttle Challenger honored us by the manner in which they lived their lives. We will never forget them, nor the last time we saw them, this morning, as they prepared for their journey and waved goodbye and 'slipped the surly bonds of earth' to 'touch the face of God.'"[9]

We are protective of our language. In the early days of the United States, Britain looked down upon American English, even panning Thomas Jefferson, author of the Declaration of Independence and arguably one of the greatest writers in American history, for his use of the word "belittle," which appears in his *Notes on Virginia* in 1787. (Note: Jefferson is credited with coining the word "belittle" and over 100 other words, although the honor may have come Tom's way because his usage of certain terms marked the first time a lexicographer took note of it.)

"*Belittle!* What an expression!" read a column in the *European Magazine and London Review*. "It may be an elegant one in Virginia, and even perfectly intelligible; but for our part, all we can do is, to guess at its meaning. For shame, Mr. Jefferson! … O spare us, we beseech you, our mother-tongue."[10]

In 2017, U.S. Senator Elizabeth Warren was admonished by the Senate because she wouldn't stop talking when she was asked to be silent. "Nevertheless, she persisted," said Senate Majority Leader Mitch McConnell as he explained why Warren was reprimanded.[11]

That incident came to mind when thinking about the grammatical and xenophobic tsk-tsk Jefferson received. During the emergence of American English, young Noah Webster undertook the arduous task of writing his own book on English grammar, despite the fact that he was entering into a market that was thoroughly flooded with competition. Well-established British grammar books ("grammars," as they were called back then) had taken root in American classrooms. Webster, like Warren over 200 years later, persisted.[12]

In Webster's time, a British scholar wrote that our langue is a relapse into semi-barbarism. We may be barbaric, but we love to study, analyze, explain, bend, and stretch the language.

We stand by the uniqueness of our language, and we're a bit xenophobic ourselves, sometimes insisting American English be the first (if not the only) choice of communication. In 2006, the owner of Geno's Steaks in South Philadelphia, Joseph Vento, posted a sign outside his establishment saying, "This is America. When ordering, 'speak English'." His position caused a brief media stir, but Mr. Vento held his ground. "[T]hey would have to handcuff me and take me out because I am not taking [the sign] down," he told a reporter.[13]

It took nearly 10 years, but the sign was eventually removed. While it was there, however, a film crew from Britain was in Philadelphia and decided to try some Philly cuisine and ordered cheesesteaks from Geno's. One member of the film crew had grown up in Liverpool, England, and his birthright vocabulary was the Scouse dialect, better known as Liverpool English or "cockney." While he spoke a formal style of English, he could easily revert to his heavy cockney accent, and he decided to have some fun by putting said accent to full use when the crew visited Geno's. His exchange was captured by a cleverly hidden video camera, held by another member of the crew.

"Oy," he shouted through the customer service window at Geno's, "Aye am speakin' fukin' English!!" Somehow, he managed to order his cheesesteak while giving an American payback for Thomas Jefferson's "belittle."

(Footnote: This anecdote was never reported in the press. I know about it only because said film crew was in town to film an interview with a University of Pennsylvania professor. When they finished the interview, they asked the UPenn public relations representative—some bum named Joe Diorio—where they could buy a genuine Philly Cheesesteak. Said P.R. pro then egged them on to pull this stunt. Was secretly filming Joey Vento a good idea? Probably not. Nevertheless, they persisted.)

Our fascination with intricate aspects of our language led me to examine its many quirks in *A Few Words About Words*®.

Our language, as the aforementioned citation demonstrates, is a relapse into semi-barbarism. Yet we spend an inordinate amount of time studying, analyzing, explaining, bending, and stretching the very thing we barbarize and are so barbaric about. Language is a living expression of the mind and spirit of a people, ever-changing and shifting with a standard of usage that flows with the customs of the people it serves. It continuously changes.

More than once, someone has read my newsletter about good writing and inevitably stated that it's amazing I always come up with fresh content to write about. I'm more amazed that someone thinks writing about language is so hard. It's all around us.

ABOUT THE NEWSLETTER

When I struck out on my own as a freelance advertising copywriter in the early 1990s, I knew I needed some help in generating new business. I am not a natural salesman and, therefore, could not simply make cold calls to ask people for work. I couldn't even envision myself making cold calls to prospective customers. All that would come to my mind when I'd think about cold calling is a story about country music legend Johnny Cash as described by his daughter, Roseanne. She said her father, long before his country music fame, worked for a time as a door-to-door vacuum cleaner salesman. Roseanne Cash said that after a homeowner would answer Cash's knock on the door (clearly this was back in the days when one would actually *open* the door when someone knocked), Cash proceeded with the following sales pitch:

"You don't want to buy anything, do ya?"[14]

That sounded *so* much like me. Like I said, I can't make cold calls. I also knew it could be awkward for the people being asked and those doing the asking.

I vividly remember the time a freelancer, who had approached me for work when I was working as a speech writer for DuPont, started to cry when I said I had no freelance assignments to dole out. A few years earlier, when I was working for IBM, a former employee showed up at my office—one week after they had retired—and *demanded* I hire them as a freelance writer.

In both cases I was left feeling like the mayor of Awkwardville. Those emotional and overly blunt tactics were bad form and definitely not my style.

But if flat out asking for work won't work for me, what was left?

Around the time that I tried my hand at self-employment, (Yes, I went into self-employment without a plan to find business. Otto von Bismarck is credited with saying, "God has a special providence for fools [and] drunkards."[15]) a colleague who ran a public relations agency told me he would mail news articles he found interesting to potential prospects. "It shows you are well-read and helps you keep in touch," he explained.

That was low-key, and I would not pester anyone. OK, I had the how. All I needed was the what. The answer came to me while watching an episode of *Star Trek: The Next Generation*. (Hey, I was just starting out; I wasn't that busy and had time to watch reruns.)

That iteration of the original *Star Trek* series had deftly rendered neutral a very sexist line uttered by William Shatner's Captain James T. Kirk in the original *Star Trek* television show. In the introduction of the original series, Captain Kirk would say, "To boldly go where no man has gone before."[16] But for fans of The Next Generation, or TNG, the line uttered by Patrick Stewart's Captain Jean-Luc Picard was, "To boldly go where no one has gone before."[17] Corny? Yes. Predictable? Sure, it is *Star Trek*. But it got the point across. It's also a great example of gender-neutral writing.

I put that trite observation in a homemade newsletter (it was an 8.5 by 11-inch sheet of paper), printed envelopes, and mailed this document to about 50 clients and friends. The newsletter *A Few Words About Words*® (AFWAW) was born.

And no sooner did I say, "wonder if it'll work" than I began getting incredibly positive feedback. Prospective and regular clients appreciated the brief respite from their daily grind and the fact that I wasn't begging them for work.

Nowadays, nearly 30 years into writing the newsletter, the feedback I get from readers of AFWAW is encouraging, humbling, and sometimes downright terrifying.

Encouraging: "I love your newsletter. Keep it up!"

Humbling: "Thanks to you I miss William Safire a bit less." (Or this one, more embarrassing than humbling, "I worship the ground you walk on!")

Terrifying: "Do you write *A Few Words About Words*? That's a 'must read' for me."

That last compliment truly scared me; I realized at that moment that I *have to* come up with good content from that point forward. Readers are relying on me.

Today, we live in a world where countless social media outlets populate our culture—over five billion people use Facebook, Twitter, Whatsapp, Instagram, Messenger, and other social media tools. Yet we still struggle with writing. Candidates for the local board of education confuse "loose" with "lose" (or so someone tells me via Twitter) and that is just the tip of the grammatical iceberg. Social media is often the only way we introduce ourselves. Writing "your" when you mean "you're" and "there" when you mean "they're" is the difference between getting or not getting new business, or just getting to know someone.

What is truly frustrating to me is that too many people think it's OK to have a mistake in something they write, especially if it is in a text, an email, or a social media post. I am here to tell you that it isn't OK, and the reasons are elegantly explained by Timothy Fallis, a former college professor at Hawai'i Pacific University in his presentation, "Gramma Wamma!" (I'll explain more about the name and Tim's presentation later.)

"Explain to me why this stuff is important, especially in the era of texting and snapchat and iffy thumb-typing," he writes, paraphrasing his student's laments about learning grammar. "Three reasons! You DON'T want to come off like an uneducated buffoon, you DO want to impress your reader with your precise and careful erudition, and you DO want to communicate with absolute clarity; otherwise, you're wasting your time *and* your readers' [time]."[18]

Couldn't have said it better myself.

By the way, anyone saying, "Video content is taking over the internet, so why worry about writing?" should be aware that the crux of any video is the written word. Virtually all videos began as an idea scratched on paper. *Somebody* decided to first write movie lines like, "Here's looking at you, kid," "[Luke] I am your father," and "Get your stinking paws off me, you damned dirty ape." Frankly, my dear, I don't give a damn if you disagree with me on this point. The written word is the basis for all video content.

ABOUT THE SIGN OFF IN EVERY NEWSLETTER

In the 1980s, my favorite TV show was *Hill Street Blues*, which was about a police precinct in a large midwestern city. Every episode began with the sergeant giving instructions to the police officers for the upcoming day. He would conclude his morning remarks with the line, "Let's be careful out there."[19]

I borrowed and modified the sergeant's line so that every issue of my newsletter concludes with the polite admonition, "Let's write carefully out there, people."

This book is my love letter to the written word, penned by a guy who doesn't always know what he's doing with pen in hand. While I opened by sharing how and why I am bad at grammar, this isn't a tell-all of my formative school years. My story, in that respect, is not nearly as engaging as the narrative Tara Westover shares in *Educated: A Memoir*. Instead, it is a "we're all in this together" clarion call to pay attention to what we commit to paper or keyboards. An instructor from a professional development seminar I attended once said, "Writing is not a natural act." He was *so* right. It's hard. It requires diligence, and it can take a lot of work.

So, why do we write? Because the final product can be fun, engaging, entertaining. Or, as an old friend, the late Bob Jagoda, author of the 1979 novel *Nobody Wants My Resume,* said, "We write because something inside of us says we must."

I began this book by simply cutting and pasting all the back issues of AFWAW that I could find into a single word document. I figured there was more than enough material for a book. Well, there was enough, but just putting column after column in a big, clunky document doth not make a book. Howard Stern discovered that this approach doesn't work when he wrote and published his 2019 compilation of his radio interviews in the book *Howard Stern Comes Again.* He said in that book's introduction that he thought it would be easy just to provide a running list of his interviews. It wasn't. And the book, he said, required a serious amount of original content.[20] I read Stern's book before writing this one. But did I follow his sage advice? Of course not. I learned the hard way … the same way I learned English grammar.

The columns are arranged around what seems to be logical themes, weaving in more information along the way. I limit each issue of AFWAW to around 700 words. My thinking is that someone is reading the newsletter first thing in the morning and doesn't have the time or interest to read a lengthy missive, no matter how good the content may be. In this book, I gave myself the luxury of expanding a bit more on certain subjects.

I encourage you to read this book if you were ever teased in school for not knowing the answers or if you have struggled with writing an email or interoffice memo. I offer a true layman's approach to understanding and using our language. It is a combination of columns from the popular AFWAW monthly email newsletter and blog, tied together with humor and personal anecdotes.

Let's write carefully out there, people.

1

gramma wamma

The first daily newspaper I worked for was a throwback to the days of "The Front Page." The Post Publishing Company occupied a building in downtown Bridgeport, Connecticut that, by the time I worked there in 1978, was well over 50 years old. Everyone used a manual typewriter, and the electric newswire teleprinters clacked away nonstop, churning out one story after another from the far corners of the world. The newsroom was loud, hot (there was no air conditioning), ink was so badly embedded into each desk that everyone's shirt had ink-stained elbows, and it smelled of bad cigars (Topstone cigars, made right there in Bridgeport). All that was missing was Hildy Johnson covering the police beat.

One day, a friend and co-worker discovered that the "F" key on his typewriter was no longer functional. He approached the managing editor, a dapper-dressed character whose first name was Lenny, to ask for a new typewriter … or at least one that was manufactured after 1965.

"Why do you need a new typewriter?" Lenny asked.

"The 'F' key on mine doesn't work anymore," my friend said.

After a long pause Lenny responded, "Well, don't use any words with the letter 'F in them."

Fuming ("Uming?"), my friend returned to his desk, put a sheet of paper in his typewriter, and typed out the following note, "Hey, Lenny, 'Uck you!'"

I thought about this story when a reader of *A Few Words About Words* wrote to tell me that the number '5' key on his computer doesn't work anymore, so he's constantly figuring out ways to avoid using it. That's called writing around a problem.

My friend at the newspaper eventually left his job and went on to a successful career in corporate public relations. At that moment, though, he had found a way to basically write around his grammatical roadblocks. In his case, the "fix" wouldn't be all inclusive (he would have to call it an "ix"), but he did write around the problem for at least long enough to write what we'd nowadays call a burn letter to his boss.

Writing around a problem is common. We skip words we always seem to misspell or that look wrong on the computer screen and avoid grammatical rules we just can't remember and certainly don't want to look up. Writing around a problem is, I suspect, a near universal practice among professional writers and the casual writer who sends off the occasional text message.

Personally, rather than trying to write "bureaucracy," I say "red tape." (I let my editors insert the word "bureaucracy" if they must). Rather than forming a plural possessive of a noun, I'd write "those bones belong to the dogs" instead of screwing it up by writing ... well, you get the idea.

I turned to social media to ask readers and followers what their grammatical roadblocks are and how they get around them.

"Thank goodness for spell check," one said. "The word 'curriculum' bedevils me, and I have to use it every day."

"I will go to great lengths to avoid writing 'no one,' because it never reads the way I would speak it. Just a weird situation," said a colleague, a doctoral degree holder who works for an engineering firm.

"Cinnamon," said another reader. "I spelled it wrong in a fifth-grade spelling bee, and it still gives me pause."

Trauma can do that to a writer. To this day, I clutch when I see the word "bologna" because I can still feel the laughter from my classmates when I pronounced it "bah-log-na" rather than "baloney." Instead of coming to my defense, my teacher, who I will henceforth refer to as "Miss Hoover" (check your list of characters on "The Simpsons") just buried her face in her hands and shook her head.

"I prefer saying 'no one' over 'nobody,' but I can't say why," another reader shared. "It just looks weird to me." (N.B.—the autocorrect on my PC, which I normally hate, always fixes "weird" when I accidentally write "wired." OK, Microsoft, thanks for that one.)

"I cannot write lists. I get confused over capitalization, punctuation, the whole smash. I just avoid writing lists," said another.

This is far from complete, but here is my cheat sheet for writing lists.

- Don't use numbers. Why number something unless the actual number indicates an order?
- The introductory sentence should grammatically flow into the list. Then add your bulleted list items.
- Each item in the list can be just one or multiple. Capitalize the first word of each point and use periods; if you use any other form of punctuation—commas or semicolons—then that list is just a long sentence you have broken up by using bullet points. Write, don't make layouts. That's for the graphic designers.

"Subject and verb conjugations that are right but sound wrong drive me nuts," another reader reports. Sure, singular subjects need singular verbs, but it can grate on your nerves to read, "The team lost its fourth straight game today." Perhaps a better example that I found through some online research would be, "Who left the bread out? It was I." Saying "it was I," unless you live in a very formal household, could sound off-putting to some.

"Synchronization … come on, it always looks like the 'h' should not be there. It's one of those words that, to me, just looks wrong." I hear ya, reader; it's like "bologna" for me.

"Embarrass and harass. Why does one have two 'r's' and the other does not?" This one is tricky. Some words will have a double consonant because of their pronunciation. But the use of the double consonant in some words, when compared with words that do not take the double, can cause confusion.

American English has some, shall we say, hangovers from British English affecting both meaning and spelling, all of which evolve over time but can cause confusion. Consider just some of the unique terms H.L. Mencken noted in his book, *The American Language*:

American—trash can
British—dustbin

American—bathtub
British—tub

American—candy
British—sweets

American—freight
British—goods

American—monkey wrench
British—spanner

And on and on.

Mencken wrote that the language of America in the early 1900s would be almost unrecognizable to the language used right after the Civil War.[1] That, I suspect, is a product of the passage of time and language evolving. "When I speak my native tongue in its utmost purity [while] in England, an Englishman can't understand me at all," said Mark Twain.[2]

When writing AFWAW, I spent a considerable amount of time online looking for some quick and easy workarounds to common writing problems. Sadly, the only one I found that is a sure-fire way to work is this: use the dictionary, damnit.

GRAMMA WAMMA

As I mentioned, my grasp of English grammar was virtually nonexistent when I was in grade school. When my family and I moved from Bridgeport, Connecticut to Trumbull, Connecticut, I discovered the other students at my new school, Center School, were about six months ahead of where my former classmates were at my old haunt, St. Raphael School in neighboring Bridgeport. My new classmates had their share of laughs at my grammatical shortcomings. It was entertaining for them and embarrassing for me.

(By the way, St. Raphael is now called St. Raphael Academy, and the location of Center School is now a parking lot. Who's laughing now, huh?)

Anyway, English grammar may be hard to master, so one may think a college refresher course on the basics would cause students to leave skid marks as they try to avoid this class. Surprisingly, a "Gramma Wamma" class, variations of which have been taught at the University of Hawai'i and stateside at Immaculata University, is one of the most popular classes around.

Timothy Fallis, Ph.D. taught as a doctoral student at the University of Pennsylvania, as a freshly minted Ph.D. at Immaculata University, and as a slightly seasoned professor at the University of Hawai'i; he says he encountered students whose grasp on English grammar was slippery at best. His solution was to (surprise!) teach. He developed a presentation to go over the basics.

The kids, he said, love it.

By the way, the name "Gramma Wamma" is, Fallis thinks, a play on Grammar Writing. He developed the content for his presentation but borrowed the title from a professor at the University of Hawai'i who was already using it.

Refresher lessons never hurt. Here's a few more.

PEOPLE, IT'S THE DOG

"My eight-year-old just asked me if 'Bingo' is the name of the farmer or the dog, and now I am questioning everything I thought I knew about life."

—INTERNET MEME THAT WAS MAKING ITS
WAY AROUND THE 'NET IN 2019

I chuckled when I read the above, which is an internet meme about the song, "B-I-N-G-O." You know, "There was a farmer who had a dog, and Bingo was his name, oh ..." and so on. Then, I became dismayed when I mentioned it to a few people and found little consensus.

"'Who had a dog' is a parenthetical statement, no? So maybe the farmer IS named Bingo," said more than one colleague.

To clear this up I did what everyone does: I asked Google. That was a bad idea.

Online forums like seebs.net and reddit.com offered discussion and a few pop-up advertisements for managing a barking dog but no real answer. Therefore, my next step was to take a deep breath, dig deep in my memory banks, and diagram the sentence.

Stop laughing. It worked.

For starters, I had to reteach myself how to diagram a sentence. It could be argued that, even more than algebra, diagramming a sentence is that one piece of knowledge from our school days that we will never have to use after we learn it. So, off to YouTube I went doing the self-education thing.

Diagramming a sentence represents basic grammar tactics.

(I kinda knew this, but YouTube confirmed it for me. Hey, I said I have to look up *everything*.) You identify the elements of the sentence: nouns (farmer, dog, name, Bingo), verbs (had, was), pronouns (his, who), adverbs (there), conjunctions (and), articles (a). Then, lay out subject, verb, and direct object on a horizontal line. Adjectives, prepositional phrases, and conjunctions go on angled lines below—to show how they flow in the sentence. The first thing you discover by doing that is the subject of the sentence is the farmer, the dog is a direct object, and Bingo works as an adjective to modify the direct object.

The result is confirmation that the dog's name is Bingo. Below is the actual diagram. Go ahead and critique me; I haven't done this since the fourth grade.

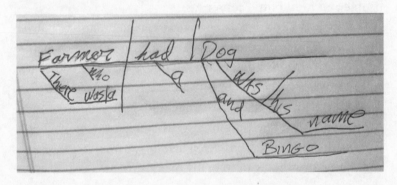

Besides, everybody knows the farmer's name is "Old MacDonald," E-I-E-I-O.

EFFECT OR AFFECT—HAVEN'T WE GONE OVER THIS BEFORE?
"English is a polyglot, messy, terrible language," Fallis tells his students. "Get over your disappointment and learn how to deal with it!"

Perhaps the most frequent request readers of AFWAW send my way (I don't actually count how many requests I get) is to explain the difference between *affect* and *effect*. Rather than speaking from the authoritative podium, I'll again turn to Tim Fallis who addresses that head-on in a writing class for his students.

In his Gramma Wamma presentation, Fallis explains that affect the *verb* means to impact or change. Affect the *noun* refers to someone's disposition as reflected in their expression or posture. Conversely, effect the *verb* is to bring about or make happen, and effect the *noun* is the result of a change. He also notes that affect the noun and effect the verb are rarely used.[3]

But we don't always listen to our teachers, do we? While watching television, I saw an on-screen graphic saying the COVID-19 pandemic was "effecting the meat industry." The day before someone on ESPN mentioned that professional football free agency was effecting the National Football League in ways not seen before.

If the pandemic is creating change in the meat industry, and said change is still in progress, then the pandemic is "affecting" the meat industry. In the same vein, NFL free agency will indeed change teams—some for the better, some for the worse—and therefore free agency is "affecting" the league. We should know by week two or three of the season what the "effect" of said change is.

But English being English, there *are* exceptions where affect is a noun and effect is a verb. As in, "Protestors want to effect change and reopen the country," or when one wants to express a feeling as in, "The patient had a flat affect during their COVID-19 therapy session."

And, yes, "affected" can be an adjective, as in, "Dr. Fauci

expressed affected abstraction when describing the pandemic." It is easy to understand why there is often so much confusion.

So many of my readers think of me as a walking grammatical encyclopedia. Trust me when I say I am not. I always look this stuff up. Therefore, on this subject, my counsel is to remember affect = verb/effect = noun for most uses, and don't be reluctant to check Google or, preferably, some other reference.

I NEED TO FACILITATE THE END OF THIS WORD

Mea culpa, I give print and broadcast journalists more than their share of grief for grammatical errors. While I honestly try to lay off as much as possible, I cannot let pass the bromance that news reporters—at the national and local level—have with using the word "facility." The overload was particularly annoying to the ears during a summer of 2017 story where pipe bombs were being sent via the United States Postal Service to high-profile Democratic party members and their supporters. The news was overflowing with the overuse of the word "facility." I heard "mail facility," "bomb disposal facility," and "investigation facility." Gloriosky, folks, how about "post office," "safe disposal site," and "crime lab." I figured the local sports report would be all clear, but Nissan Stadium, home of the Tennessee Titans of the National Football League, was referred to as a—you got it—"sports facility."

And it's not TV news that's overdoing it. On August 18, 2020, *The Tennessean* reported that Vanderbilt University Medical Center will not build a large medical center in the town of Murfreesboro, Tennessee and will instead approve construction of "a much smaller facility planned by a competing company."[4]

And a January 23, 2020, story from *The Tennessean* about

a new sports practice center Belmont University will build uses the term "facility" to describe the center six times in a paltry 120-word story.[5]

On September 7, 2020, I did a Google news search for the word "facility" in news stories. It took Google .33 seconds to return 155 *million* hits. Methinks someone facilitates the use of "facility" a bit too much.

Granted, the word "facility" does mean a "place, amenity, or piece of equipment provided for a particular purpose," so it should be acceptable when talking about a building designed for a particular purpose. But "facility" also means restroom, option, service, or a natural aptitude.

By that measure, "facility" is way too broad a term and is bandied about too much. The online dictionary of idioms says "bandied about" means to make frequent and casual or (and here's the one I like) *frivolous* use of a name, word, or idea. In other words, it's lazy writing … whether you are working for a news organization or not.

DON'T "VERB THE NOUNS"

The local TV news anchor was delivering breaking news about the arrest of a shooting suspect and said the following on live TV: "Our news team is efforting new information as we speak," meaning everyone was still gathering facts.

In that moment, the anchor "verbed" a noun. This is what grammarians refer to as denominalization or randomly changing nouns into verbs. This happens a lot. Thanks to social media "friend" is now a noun and a verb. Still there's something not quite right when it seems overdone. Many of us don't fruit our beer, as an old TV advertisement for light beer once said ("Men of the Square Table," a great series of commercials starring Burt Reynolds. You can YouTube it. Oops! I verbed a noun.), so unless we really know our audience, let's not verb nouns unnecessarily. You can and should facilitate your writing some other way. (See what I did there?)

CHAMPING, CHOMPING … JUST GET ON WITH IT ALREADY!

A television reporter was talking about how eager restaurant owners in Nashville are to reopen after being closed due to community-wide health concerns and said business owners are "chomping at the bit" to get their doors open.

I am a former horse owner (I thought I could make extra money by buying and selling them. Please do not get me started on *that* topic.), and I believe the correct term is "champing" rather than "chomping." To champ at something is defined on dictionary.com as to bite on a bit impatiently. A "bit" is the piece of metal inserted into a horse's mouth, held on either end by the rein.

Was the reporter wrong? Not necessarily. Urban Dictionary notes that "chomping at the bit" is accepted as a term for impatient and eager, like a child on Christmas morning.[6] Therefore, if we continue to accept that language is always evolving—and we do accept that, 'K? (Whoops! I used slang!)—then the reporter was on firm grammatical ground.

Let's write carefully out there, people.

2

typos and proofreading

TYPOS BEDEVIL US ALL

Typographical errors, more commonly known as "typos," really fry my cheese. (That's an urban slang term for piss me off; yeah, I could say piss me off, but I like the slang term.) Because I am historically bad at grammar, if I made a typo while writing, my parochial school upbringing would leave me feeling like I am the only person who makes typos, and, therefore, I am the worst person in the world. Mother Superior from Saint Raphael's school in Bridgeport, Connecticut, this neurosis on my part is all your fault. No takebacks.

While the nuns from my elementary school days only mildly scarred me, I am paranoid about typos. Mostly because it seems to be easy for one (or more) to evade my watchful eye.

Most of the time, when someone learns I am a writer, they

wrongly assume I am a natural at catching mistakes. That's one of two common misconceptions people have about writers and editors, besides thinking we never make grammatical mistakes (I'm not touching the topic of mistakes in content).

We all make mistakes. "You never realize how many people read your content till you make a mistake," says Holly McCall, editor-in-chief of the *Tennessee Lookout* news site. "At least they are reading [you]. I don't take that lightly."

I am no different than any other writer. I must read and re-read text to be sure there are no typos or grammatical errors. And then sometimes mistakes still get through.

Do I make mistakes when I write? Boy, *do* I?

Because my knowledge of English grammar is largely self-taught, and because my bad eyesight makes it really easy to commit a typo, I live in abject fear of sending all issues of AFWAW to its 7,000-plus readers with mistakes in it.

Long before hitting "send," I proofread the living daylights out of it.

I use the proofreading services of several close friends—my younger sister, a librarian (I say that since it seems to give her some proofreading street-cred. She could be a WWE wrestler, and she'd still be good at proofreading), and a talented young writer, Michelle, who worked for me at Harcum College and later at the University of Pennsylvania. (Yes, I hired her twice. Michelle is THAT good. One time, in the newsletter, I wrote that *The Chicago Manual of Style* has over 1,000 pages of information on writing and formatting. She pointed out that the 15th edition has precisely 956 pages of information, including the index.) I also randomly select a reader and send them a "preview" of the newsletter as a courtesy, inserting a sneaky "and let me know if you catch a typo" request into the newsletter. It's heartening to see how many people respond positively.

Despite that triple—sometimes quadruple—effort of getting extra eyeballs on the newsletter, mistakes get through. When that happens, readers are not shy about pointing them out.

Proofreading and editing can be a lonely battle. I recall a painful experience from my days working at a public relations agency, when I was not only a newcomer, but the only person on the staff who had worked for a big corporation. I was coming fresh from six years at IBM, and my wardrobe comprised dark suits, white shirts, and various striped neckties. It's safe to say my co-workers didn't dress like me. My daily outfits made me "the stuffy one" on the staff, and one co-worker took delight in teasing me and looking for every opportunity to belittle my status.

After writing and sending a memo to a client and copying some of my co-workers, the smart-aleck I referred to in the previous paragraph sent his copy back to me, pointing out that the second to last word in my memo contained a typo. "Aw," this person wrote, "and you were sooooo close." Sarcasm was dripping from every word.

I laughed, but I also was downright embarrassed. I still get upset when I catch typos in my writing, and I'm a grammar grump about mistakes I see elsewhere. (My wife refuses to let me hold a pen while reading menus in restaurants.) A writer's battle against typos can be likened to a manufacturer's effort to achieve six-sigma quality. We're trying to ensure there are no mistakes for every six million words we write. That's basically impossible, but we still try. And mistakes creep through.

YES, EVEN *I* MAKE MISTAKES

If this book's description of my grammatical skills did not leave an impression on you, then let me reiterate that I am bad a grammar. Bad enough that I need multiple proofreaders to review my work. Bad enough that I still make my share of mistakes. I am the living embodiment of the internet meme, "I do my best proofreading after I hit send."

In one issue of the newsletter, I introduced a paragraph by saying, "Less anyone think." A "shame on you" from a reader hit my email inbox at warp speed. "The word is Lest, an (sic) diminished form of 'unless' … Get your grammar straight first; then deliver your punch," wrote said reader, in no uncertain terms.

Words hurt, folks, but I stand corrected. "Lest" means with the intention of preventing something. It is used negatively to introduce a clause expressive of an action or occurrence. Therefore, with my tail metaphorically placed between my legs, I corrected the offending passage in the archived version of the newsletter.

In another newsletter, I accidentally placed an asterisk denoting a footnote *before* the period at the end of a sentence, which prompted this query from a reader, "I saw your use of an asterisk. Am I doing something wrong myself?" This broke my heart; I had left a reader who believed I am a grammar guru thinking he had been making the mistake all along. I'm a firm believer that it's better to ask for forgiveness rather than permission, so I did an immediate *mea culpa* and again called out my own mistake in the next issue.

Another reader, an old colleague from my agency days, caught an errant "of" in one issue of the newsletter and privately messaged me about the mistake. "Isn't it weird how an editor's eye fixates when it doesn't need to and doesn't when it does?" she said.

I genuinely appreciate it when someone notes a mistake. It was Tim Sullivan, a late 19th/early 20th century New York politician, who said, "I don't care what they say about me as long as they spell my name right."[1] I say I am just glad they're reading the newsletter.

PROOFREAD, PLEASE

Example One: The day before the Kansas City Chiefs were to host the Tennessee Titans in the National Football League's divisional playoffs, an ABC affiliate had the following on-screen graphic: "57000 (sic) tickets remain available." Really? Arrowhead Stadium in Kansas City holds 78,000 people, so that's a *lot* of extra tickets. Methinks someone overdid the zeroes.

Example Two: An NBC affiliate reporting on the hearings for President Trump's first impeachment trial in Washington, D.C. posted a graphic that read, "Republicans say investigation is heresay." Is it hearsay that language skills are eroding?

Example Three: Me (yes, me). In one newsletter, I said the founder of the Apostrophe Protection Society would "rage" war on misuse of the punctuation. While he may indeed be in a rage, he was actually WAGING war. Name the time and place, and I'll fall on the proverbial sword.

THE CURSE OF WRITING IN A HURRY

When I was a newspaper reporter, I would remind people that reporters don't write headlines. That job falls to an editor back in the newsroom. That was my defense if my reporting was berated by a local politician who had only read the headline, which they did not like, but not my story which, had they bothered to read it, they surely would have loved.

Headlines are written by copy desk editors who are usually in a hurry because they are under pressure of a looming deadline; deadlines that are made even shorter by us reporters who turn their copy in at the last second. (For years I have told clients, "Don't tell me to take my time on this project because I *will*.") Headlines on television news are sometimes referred to as the "lower third," or the text that you see as an overlay on the primary image. It appears at the bottom of the television screen, although it doesn't necessarily take up one third of the screen. It also is sometimes called a "news crawl." In any case, it comprises news nuggets that are written in a hurry. And just like newspaper headlines, sometimes mistakes can be made when writing text for the lower third.

In that case, ABC News gets a Mulligan for a lower third that appeared on May 26, 2018. ("Mulligan," by the way, is a term popularized by President Dwight D. Eisenhower. He was golfing and hit a bad tee shot, so he decided to give himself a "do over." Who's going to argue that with the commander in chief?[2])

Anyway, the "lower third" that day said, "Hugh Grant's Married."[3]

Hugh Grant's married … what? The name "Grant's" as constructed, is possessive. But with a deadline looming, it probably was not easy to remember to say, "Hugh Grant gets married." More than a quarter-century after starring in "Four Weddings and a Funeral," he catches up and really does get married.

Addendum—Another example that proves writers don't write headlines, and editors often write them in a hurry—sometimes in an extreme hurry—happened in Nashville when _The Tennessean_ printed a story about how toy manufacturer Lego would begin making hospital safety masks rather than its trademark plastic building blocks. The story was written by a reporter with Gannett, the company that owns _The Tennessean_ and multiple other local/regional newspapers. The headline, though, was written by someone at _The Tennessean_. Someone on deadline. Someone in a hurry. Someone who wrote (and I am not making this up), "Lego shits gears to make face masks." That's both grammatically offensive and, if true, a really painful way to make face masks, _and_ it might explain why it takes so long to get hospital safety masks to the open market. All those gear teeth that must pass through … well, you get the idea.

We all know someone who is irked by typos. One example that I found on Twitter sums up why it's so important to be mindful of them.

"I've been working on my snark, but I'm going to explode if I don't say something: if you are running for office on an education platform, please learn the difference in (sic?) 'loose' and 'lose.' The end," said _Tennessee Lookout_ editor-in-chief Holly McCall. She did not identify the offending politician.

"It's not that I'm out to shame someone," McCall later said. "But, honestly, if you are running for office, you should be held to a higher standard. It isn't just about proofreading and checking your copy. Someone should know grammar and know the difference between loose and lose. I am not the only person who will be judging."

For the record, according to *Merriam-Webster* …

- Loose: not firmly or tightly fixed in place.[4]
- Lose: be deprived of or cease to have or retain (something).[5]

You're welcome, and we need to write carefully out there because a typo will eventually get us, as content from the following issue of AFWAW demonstrates.

SURVIVING A WORD TSUNAMI

Somewhere in the history of IBM there is someone—probably retired now—who knows better than most how typos can ruin your day.

In 1985, IBM gave each of its 430,000 employees a business card-size document listing all the company holidays (New Year's Day to Christmas) for the coming year. This was pre-internet so there was no web page for that information. Everyone who worked for the company, therefore, could look at this card and see that one of the holidays for the upcoming year was Thanksgiving, which would be on **THURDSAY, November 27**.

Ow.

(No, I was not the person who created that document, but I feel their pain. And nearly 40 years later, I still have the card. I keep it as a reminder.)

Typos happen to all of us. Sometimes they're more prominent than others. "It's you versus a tsunami of words," a supervisor once told me. "Eventually, one that's spelled wrong is going to get past you."

We should all have such an understanding manager. Today there is texting, social media, and 24-hour news cycles, so that tsunami of words is bigger than ever. We need a plan to proof-read our writing. Here's one systematic way to do that.

For starters, the moment you finish writing something, put it aside. Time is your friend, even if a deadline is breathing down your neck. Play a round of solitaire on your smart phone. Anything other than looking at what you wrote. Sandie Giles, author of *How to Proofread Your Own Writing*, says impatience and familiarity are two factors that are detrimental to your ability to proofread. A bit of separation can help you catch that errant mistake.[6]

Next, plan on reading your document at least *four* times, looking for specific things each time. Yes, four times. Do not just say, "I'll carefully proofread it." *How* will you do the proofreading? A plan spells out several reads you should do for your document and identifies what you will read and what you should look for.

First pass—misspellings. A colleague who worked for the Associated Press said he reads with the assumption that every word is misspelled. While you may not have to be that xtreme (See what I just did there?), focus exclusively on how each word is spelled.

Second pass—punctuation. Do you have the period or other punctuation inside or outside quote marks? (Hint: they go inside.) Is that semicolon necessary, or can you break the sentence in two? Quick *mea culpa*. I love using semicolons. It makes me think I'm smarter than I really am.

Third pass—formatting. A generation ago Strunk and White in *The Elements of Style* advised us to "choose a suitable design and hold to it."[7] Are any subheads formatted consistently? Is each paragraph indentation the same? In lists, do you use bullets or numbers? And in those lists, are you using parallel construction with an action verb to start each point (as in "build," "wait," "stop," etc.)?

Fourth pass—have someone else read it. I have several friends and colleagues who proofread my monthly newsletter, *A Few Words About Words*®, to be sure it's right. And occasionally mistakes do get through.

Now, for those of you who have recoiled in horror, saying, "Read it *four times*?? Who has that kind of time?" Well, then here is one more trick I learned that usually works. Change the font on your document before your proofread it. It will trick your brain into thinking you are reading something new, and those wayward grammatical errors or innocent misspellings will most likely stand out.

Professional communicators put a lot of effort into their messages. How those messages are proofread is the final step to make our work successful.

Let's write—and proofread—carefully out there, people.

3

punctuation

LYNNE TRUSS, author of the great book *Eats, Shoots & Leaves*, is credited with saying, "There are two kinds of people in the world; those who use the Oxford Comma and those who do not. Never get in-between these people when drink has been taken."[1]

I sympathize, and I am firmly on the side of those who use a comma after the penultimate item in a list of three or more. And not just because I like being able to use words like "penultimate." It's more because I believe—heck, I am *sure*—that every time someone does not use the Oxford Comma, a puppy dies. Begrudgingly, though, I acknowledge that the rules of punctuation are as much a subject of debate and are as much in flux as any other part of our language.

Over 100 years ago H.L. Mencken wrote, "All of us, no matter how careful our speech habits, loosen the belt a bit, so to speak, when we talk familiarly to our fellows, and pay a good deal less heed to precedents and proprieties, perhaps, than we ought to."[2] To paraphrase Mencken in today's slang, we all let our grammatical guard down from time to time.

Remember, though, I said language is our perpetual shiny object. Society obsesses over it, which explains this tweet from @WilliamAder:

Therapist: So what's troubling you?

Me: There should be a comma between Hey and Jude.

He's right. There also needs to be a comma after "So," but there I go digressing again.

Merriam-Webster defines the word "hey" as an interjection or an abrupt remark. It is frequently used to first get someone's attention, then make a statement. *Merriam-Webster's* own example from the *Arizona Republic* is, "Hey, Tigs, the 80s are over, man. Time to lose that orange Mohawk."[3]

Interestingly, Lennon and McCartney got it right in the song's final stanza, writing "Na-na-na-na, hey, Jude."[4]

DON'T TOUCH MY COMPOUND MODIFIER

The Oxford comma is not the only punctuation topic that will get people up in arms. Early in the summer of 2019, the Associated Press decreed that compound modifiers no longer require a hyphen if the modifier is commonly recognized as one phrase and if the meaning is clear and unambiguous, as in "first quarter touchdown" rather than "first-quarter touchdown." If Twitter is any indication, the change was not well-received (well received?). One tweet summed it up this way, "No offense, but burn in hell." Another said, "Over my still-warm dead body."

Welp, power to the people. The @APStylebook listened. In a tweet a little more than a month later, the AP said, "Upon further reflection and thanks to your feedback, we're reversing that decision."[5] That's a fourth-quarter comeback, for sure.

THE APOSTROPHE PROTECTION SOCIETY LIVES! SORTA.
Every year has its share of comings and goings. In 2019, grammar aficionados like myself initially mourned the departure of the Apostrophe Protection Society (APS), then cheered when the group apparently made a comeback. Or so we hope.

The APS was created in 2001 by a retired journalist in the United Kingdom named John Richards to, as he explains, "defend the much-abused punctuation mark." For 18 years, Richards would wage war—no, I don't know how—against usage like "apples's for sale," or "ladies fashions." But Richards, at age 96, said the war is over.[6]

"When I first set it up, I would get about 40 emails or letters a week from people all over the world," he told the BBC. "[N]owadays, I hardly get anything."[7]

But shortly after Richards's (yes, "Richards's." That's how you use an apostrophe to make a name that ends in "s" possessive … unless you are using the AP Stylebook, which argues "Richards'" is also correct.) post, the Apostrophe Protection Society website had a 600-fold increase in traffic. "The APS website is NOT closing down!" says a message on the APS website. I'm not sure Richards wrote that but reports of the death of the Apostrophe Protection Society are, to quote Mark Twain, "greatly misquoted."

We should never give in to bad grammar, even if a 96-year-old man says he is throwing in the towel. There are grammatical practices or phrases that should go away forever. The proper use of the apostrophe is not one of them.

ASTERISKS RATHER THAN QUOTE MARKS

Anybody notice the trend of using a double asterisk in place of quote marks? A recent tweet by Kelly Rippin, a TV news anchor in Cincinnati read, "… explains has more on how the Grand Jury came to this decision …" A few minutes later the anchor tweeted a correction, writing "has more on** no need for the word 'explains' there. I'm typing too fast and needed to proofread!"

Because I'm old (there, I said it for you), I would have written, "has more 'on' …" which seems to be the accepted construction. Or so I thought before I asked my social media hive mind.

"Hive mind," by the way, is a derivative description of groupthink. Its genesis goes back to bees working together in a hive or perhaps the deadly efficiency of the Borg on *Star Trek*. Or is it *Star Trek***?

The hive mind from my social media feeds provide some interesting theories.

One suggestion is that the double asterisk doesn't turn into a bullet point as the Microsoft Word application tends to do (after typing an asterisk and then hitting the space bar), so a double asterisk stays a double asterisk (take that, Microsoft). Another member of the hive mind opined, "I think it's to say, 'look look look oops!' rather than, 'look oops.'"

"You know, I think it dates to the AOL Instant Messenger days," Rippin says. "To correct something, you used to put a "*"" before or after the correction." She might be on to something. In the "old internet" days that Linguist Gretchen McCulloch describes in her book, *Because Internet: Understanding the New Rules of Language*, symbols like the asterisk were a part of HTML coding, so it could be a holdover. McCulloch also describes the use of asterisks as a kind of decorative typography.[8]

Here's something else to consider. *The Chicago Manual of Style*, my bible for most things grammatical, says an asterisk is used for footnotes where it delineates different points in footnotes, AND, interestingly, offers the following advice:

Other ways to break text. "Where a break stronger than a paragraph but not as strong as a subhead is required, a set of asterisks … may be inserted between paragraphs."[9] In other words, an asterisk can be used as a form of emphasis. Look**, this is important, OK?

HOLIDAY CARD GRAMMAR DRIVES ME CRAZY

I'm going to bypass holiday discussion topics like how it's a great time to reconnect with family or how it's an equally great time to grab a drink *because* we are reconnecting with family (that last statement was the crux of a magazine ad for scotch whiskey). Instead, I'm going to drive right to the point: the holidays are a great time to drive me crazy with the inappropriate use of apostrophes.

Honest to goodness, folks. I probably missed the lesson about apostrophes because I was changing schools as my family moved to a new school district, or my ADHD prevented me from paying attention. But were ALL OF YOU moving? Is ADHD that pervasive? (OK, some will argue that it is.)

What follows is one of my first holiday editions of AFWAW,

and it generated multiple "thank you" notes from readers, including one reader who said, "This is the answer to my prayers." (I would have asked for world peace, but that's just me. Yes, I am digressing.)

NOT A CREATURE WAS STIRRING, EXCEPT FOR THOSE DARN APOSTROPHES

The holiday season is upon us. Or at least it has been since late September when my local Walmart put out its first Christmas decorations. But more important than the over-commercialization of the holiday is what showed up in my mailbox the other day. It was a Christmas card with the following written inside:

"Happy holidays! We love the Diorio's."

Wait! Love the Diorio's ... WHAT? Our humor? Our address? The way I make mountains out of grammatical molehills?

I take issue with the last item. It seems knowing how to make one's last name plural has gone the way of waiting until your second slice of apple pie after Thanksgiving dinner before playing any Vince Guaraldi Trio Christmas music. (Guaraldi wrote the well-known music for many of the Charlie Brown television specials.)

"Diorio's," as it appeared on the card, is *possessive*. Simply adding an "s" at the end, Diorios, makes it plural. I suspect the person who sent this card—who is no doubt removing me from their Christmas card list as they read this—meant to say "Diorios" rather than "Diorio's."

Since it appears to be *that hard* to make someone's last name plural rather than possessive, and I suspect more than a few of us will be sending Christmas (OK, *HOLIDAY)* cards, I offer to you a (hopefully definitive guide) to pluralizing your last name.

LAST LETTER(S) OF LAST NAME	WHAT SHOULD YOU ADD TO MAKE IT PLURAL?	DOES IT NEED AN APOSTROPHE?
a, b, c, d, e, f, g, h (see exceptions below), i, j, k, l, m, n, o, p, q, r, t, u, v, w, y	An 's.' That's it.	Nope.
s, x, z, ch, sh	An 'es.'	See above.

Avoid adding "ies" to pluralize anything. And don't ask, "What if my name is an irregular noun?" If it's your name, then it isn't an irregular noun.

MARK TWAIN'S FINAL WORD(S) ON PUNCTUATION

Mark Twain was particular about his use of punctuation. In the *Autobiography of Mark Twain,* he said his punctuation is "the one thing I am inflexibly particular about ... it's got more real variety about it than any other accomplishment I possess."[10] Rumor has it he also once wrote a story or short essay and left all the punctuation marks in the footnotes for the reader to sort out. Scholar Cecelia Watson, author of *Semicolon: The Past, Present, and Future of a Misunderstood Mark,* wrote that she was unsuccessful in finding the story that is missing punctuation.[11]

Still, reports of Twain's antics are not highly exaggerated, and

I attempted to confirm this interesting rumor. I checked with Laura Skandera Trombley, Ph.D., president of Southwestern University and a well-known Twain scholar. She confessed that she, too, was not familiar with this anecdote but said Twain was quite particular about punctuation, especially if a printer tried changing his work. She shared a letter Twain wrote in 1897 where he complained about printer edits by Spottiswoode & Co., a large (and still in business) printer in London:

> "I give it up. These printers pay no attention to my punctuation. Nine-tenths of the labor & vexation put upon me by Messrs. Spothiswoode (sic) & co consists in annihilating their ignorant & purposeless punctuation & restoring my own.
>
> This latest batch, beginning with page 145 & running to page 192 starts out like all that went before it—with my punctuation ignored & their insanities substituted for it. I have read two pages of it—I can't stand any more. If they will restore my punctuation themselves & then send the purified page to me I will read it for errors of grammar & construction—that is enough to require of an author who writes as legible a hand as I do, & who knows more about punctuation in two minutes than any damned bastard of a proof-reader can learn in two centuries.
>
> Conceive of this tumbl-bug interesting himself in my punctuation—which is none of his business & with which he has nothing to do—& then instead of correcting mis-spelling which is in his degraded line, striking a mark under the word & silently confessing that he doesn't know what the hell to do with it! The damned half-developed foetus!

But this is the Sabbath Day, & I must not continue in this worldly vein.

Ys
SLC

P.S.—These are not revises—they are first-proofs, & bad ones at that."[12]

"Twain was very proud of his punctuation, as well he should have been," writes Susan Harris, Ph.D., a Twain scholar from the University of Kansas. "I learned a lot from studying his use of semicolons."

FLASH QUIZ (STOP COMPLAINING, IT'S EASY)

Look at the sentences below and decide what the correct punctuation should be. Like Twain reportedly once did, I have placed all of the necessary punctuation—plus a few more that probably don't need to be there—below the sentences.

The first one:

im saying it because its true inside of us we both know you belong with victor youre part of his work the thing that keeps him going if that plane leaves the ground and youre not with him youll regret it maybe not today maybe not tomorrow but soon and for the rest of your life

From the movie, *Casablanca*

The second one:

> well im not gonna leave you alone i want you to get mad i don't want you to protest i dont want you to riot i dont want you to write to your congressman because i wouldnt know what to tell you to write i dont know what to do about the depression and the inflation and the russians and the crime in the street all I know is that first youve got to get mad youve got to say im a human being god dammit my life has value
>
> so i want you to get up now i want all of you to get up out of your chairs i want you to get up right now and go to the window open it and stick your head out and yell im as mad as hell and im not gonna take this anymore

From the movie, *Network*

The third (and last) one:

> its not who i am underneath but what i do that defines me

From the movie, *Batman Begins*

Correct Answers:

> I'm saying it because it's true. Inside of us, we both know you belong with Victor. You're part of his work, the thing that keeps him going. If that plane leaves the ground and you're not with him, you'll regret it. Maybe not today. Maybe not tomorrow, but soon and for the rest of your life.

Well, I'm not gonna leave you alone. I want you to get mad! I don't want you to protest. I don't want you to riot - I don't want you to write to your congressman because I wouldn't know what to tell you to write. I don't know what to do about the depression and the inflation and the Russians and the crime in the street. All I know is that first you've got to get mad. You've got to say, 'I'm a HUMAN BEING, God damn it! My life has VALUE!' So I want you to get up now. I want all of you to get up out of your chairs. I want you to get up right now and go to the window. Open it, and stick your head out, and yell, 'I'M AS MAD AS HELL, AND I'M NOT GOING TO TAKE THIS ANYMORE!'

It's not who I am underneath... but what I do ... that defines me.

Let's write (and punctuate) carefully out there, people.

4

write what you mean and mean what you write

THE VERY FIRST ONE

As mentioned in my introduction, I was nervous as heck when I started writing AFWAW. Who would want to read it? Could I even come up with content that was halfway decent?

In my nightmares, I imagined someone getting the newsletter in the mail—it was sent via U.S. Postal mail in the early days—and they would say something like, "Who is this guy, and what's he trying to prove?" I thought long and hard about the content of those early newsletters, especially the first one. The newsletter was my sole tool for introducing myself to prospective freelance writing clients and would frequently be the only thing they had that reminded them of me. If I sent them something they perceived as dribble, then my chances of getting freelance work went way down.

Firsts should be memorable. How many bars do we visit where there is a framed dollar bill on the wall, signifying the first dollar that business ever earned? We feel the same way about our first paycheck, even as we wonder "Who is this FICA and why did he take my money?" like the character Rachel said in the very first episode of the sitcom *Friends*.[1]

People who are familiar with the comic strips like *Garfield, Peanuts,* or *Bloom County* may remember the very first edition of each of those classics.

- Garfield said, "Feed me" in response to his "owner," Jon Arbuckle, saying, "Our only thought is to entertain you."[2]
- Two characters watch Charlie Brown walk toward them. One says, "Here comes good old Charlie Brown," only to add, "How I hate him" once he is out of earshot.[3]
- And in *Bloom County* Milo's grandfather goes to a Burger King—home of the "Have it Your Way" motto—and asks for a milkshake "hold the cup."[4] Yes, I read too many comic strips.
- But there is a first time for everything. Digging through dozens of my old 3.5-inch floppy disks, I *think* what follows is the very first issue of AFWAW. It's super short because, like I said, I didn't know what to write, and I was terrified that I would offend some recipients. Please note that I have modified it a bit to comport with today's social media-focused world. I did not at that point in time have the foresight to predict Twitter.

It's also the first issue of AFWAW to use the tagline, "Let's write carefully out there, people." Yay, milestones!

BREVITY, THY NAME IS FRANKLIN

Many of us may not have the right to vote if it weren't for clear and concise writing.

During Ben Franklin's day, as he was knee-deep in the development of the United States and its Constitution, a battle raged in the Continental Congress over who gets the right to vote. Federalists insisted that you must own property to have voting rights. The Franklinites opposed this, explaining their position in long and drawn-out language. I'm afraid you'll put the book down if I include too much Colonial era lingo, so here's a snippet of what Franklin's allies argued:

> It cannot be adhered to with any reasonable degree of intellectual or moral certainty that the inalienable right man possesses to exercise his political preferences by employing his vote in referendums is rooted in anything other than man's own nature, and is, therefore, properly called a natural right.
>
> To hold, for instance, that this natural right can be limited externally by making its exercise more dependent on a prior condition of ownership of property, is to wrongly suppose that man's natural right to vote is somehow more inherent in and more dependent on the property of man than it is on the nature of man.
>
> It is obvious that such a belief is unreasonable, for it reverses the order of rights intended by nature.[5]

Ah-looo! Down here! It's OK if you glossed over all of that. Dr. Franklin was afraid the framers of the Constitution would, too.

Dr. Franklin was no social media influencer, but he knew how to put important information into easy to digest formats. Knowing that few people would wade through the aforementioned and cumbersome statement, he offered a more Tweet-friendly version. (Yes, I know there was no Twitter back then. Social media was someone yelling out the news in the town square. My statement is metaphorical.) He said, simply:

> To require property of voters leads us to this dilemma: I own a jackass: I can vote. The jackass dies: I cannot vote. Therefore, the vote represents not me but the jackass.[6]

This may not be the exact line, so please don't "@" me ... that's a social media phenomenon whereby one is inundated with messages that are along the lines of "Whadda YOU know?"

JOURNALISM: A TOUGH JOB WITH INSANE PRESSURE AND PRETTY CRAPPY PAY. ON THE OTHER HAND, EVERYBODY HATES YOU.

Here is the first line from a news story in *The Hour,* a daily newspaper in Norwalk, Connecticut: "It's gotten to the point recently where officials at the Oak Hills Golf Course are expecting to find the work of vandals on the course grounds when they conduct inspections."[7]

"It's gotten"?? OK, "it's" can be a contraction for "it has." But "It's gotten"? Yuck. How about something more direct like this: "Oak Hills Golf Course officials expect to find vandalism every day." That's simple, to the point, and no fluffy language surrounding it.

Am I being harsh on the writer? Yup. That's OK, though,

because I'm the writer of this offending opening paragraph. I wrote that story more than 40 years ago when I was a daily newspaper reporter for *The Hour*. (Sidebar: Members of the staff would refer to *The Hour* as "60 Minutes." Not because we thought we were as good as that iconic television news program, but because we knew we were *that bad*. Self-deprecation is sometimes the best humor.)

I'm sharing this old clip not for some self-flagellation, but to point out a basic tenant of writing for newspapers, websites, or broadcast. It's hard to write well when you are under a deadline.

Throughout the history of *A Few Words About Words*®, I point out examples of grammatical mistakes by my colleagues in the press. I'm not doing that to make fun of the news media. Politicians beat up the press enough, and they do not need my help, nor do I want to offer it. Fact is, while some criticism of the news media may be deserved, most of it is not.

My inclusion of journalistic mistakes here and in the newsletter is by no means meant to be a comprehensive review of errors in the press. Everybody makes mistakes when they write, as do U.S. Presidents (covfefe anyone?), teachers, great writers, and not so great writers. The biggest difference is that the press' mistakes are always out there for everyone to see and critique. "We hang our ass out there every day for people to take shots at us," an editor once told me. "It is a part of the job."

I admire everyone who works in that field, but whenever you are in a situation where you are writing every day your work will be cherry picked by the nitpickers of the world.

That said, I admit that I did mercilessly tease a professional colleague who worked in TV news. Whenever I would see him, I'd shout, "Hey, your tie is crooked," and he would invariably reach for his necktie ... even if he was wearing no tie and an open collar shirt. He would mutter a few curse words in my direction and move on.

I look upon errors I see as a teaching moment, not an indictment. The heading up above: "a tough job ... everybody basically hates you," nicely sums up how most people working in the news business feel at one time or another.

I spent my first three years out of college as a daily newspaper reporter, and that was one of the jobs on my long and unimpressive resume I enjoyed the most. And, yes, it had insane pressure, low pay, and pretty much everyone loved to second guess me at best, constantly criticize me at worst.

"You're the guy who wrote those shitty stories," a political consultant said upon meeting me for the first time. I could go on forever with similar examples, but that's really going off track. I met this consultant in the fall of 1980 when I was covering the unsuccessful congressional campaign of John A. Phillips in Connecticut. Like me, this individual was fairly new to his job, but he knew how to put a reporter on the defensive.

Earlier, I said working in news is fun because you are never bored and, if you are really lucky, you are a witness when the bad guys get caught. It was fun, and at the time I didn't mind not making much money.

Well, for a while I didn't mind the low wages. I left journalism after three years for a greener paycheck in corporate America.

I may have left the profession, but still, I hold news professionals in high esteem. I know how hard the job is. You are researching and writing about a subject you may know little or nothing about, you are doing it on the fly, and you are expected to never, ever make a mistake. I will forever maintain that is nearly impossible.

It also creates an environment for some doozy grammatical mistakes. There's the headline about a Major League Baseball pitcher who can throw with his right hand and his left hand that read, "Amphibious pitcher makes debut."[8] Or the story out of San Francisco that read, "Two cable cars have been arrested."[9] Short deadlines can easily equal mistakes. Just Google "Newspaper headline mistakes," and there is no shortage of what you will find.

But I'm not here to beat up the press. I use the newsletter to call out mistakes I see, but I don't throw reporters under the bus. Like I said, the job is hard enough without having some curmudgeon sniping at editors and reporters.

That said, the field of journalism remains a target-rich environment to find mistakes. And brevity is not always a virtue. To wit:

JEFFERSON DAVIS AND A BOTTLE OF BOURBON
The Commonwealth of Kentucky, in an effort to eradicate images of the Confederacy from the hallways of government, recently removed a statue of Jefferson Davis from the state capitol building. In doing so, workers discovered the base of the statue held an old bourbon bottle with a note inside of it.[10] The note in a bottle had been there since the statue was installed in the 1930s. One television reporter said it was "A bottle of bourbon with a note in it." A more accurate description would have been to say *an empty bourbon bottle with a note in it.* I wonder if the note's message was, "I.O.U. one full bottle of bourbon."

THAT'S A DANGEROUS-SOUNDING CAR FACTORY

An anchor on the local network affiliate said someone was shot "by a passing Dodge Charger with a .45 caliber pistol." I wonder if that .45 is an option or factory installed?

That's it. Nothing more to see here folks.

BREVITY IS ALSO THE PATH TO CONFUSION

Example 1: Opponents of the Oxford comma ranted over usage that appeared on the website *News of Fashion*. Citing a story in *Vogue* magazine, the website's headline read, "Cardi B on Raising Her Daughter, Bernie Sanders, and Coordinating Outfits."[11] They complained that the usage of the Oxford comma makes it look like Bernie Sanders was Cardi B's daughter.

With respect to the naysayers, they're wrong. If I write, "My daughter, Hannah, and Chelsea rented a house in Pensacola, Florida," then one might mistakenly think my daughter's name is Hannah. But if I add a sentence, "The three of them had a good time," then you know my daughter is *not* named Hannah. The problem is not with the Oxford comma but with a lack of enough detail.

Example 2: The subhead on *The New York Times* October 17, 2019 story about the death of U.S. Rep. Elijah Cummings read, "A son of sharecroppers, he fought tirelessly for his hometown, Baltimore, and became a key figure in the investigation of President Trump."[12] In this case, "Baltimore" is intended to be a parenthetical statement, but one could confuse the headline to be saying that he fought for two cities—his hometown *and* Baltimore. This could easily be cleared up by saying "he fought tirelessly for his hometown of Baltimore."

Brevity is always good, but there can be exceptions. It is especially bothersome in social media where brevity often breeds snarkiness rather than insight.

That's not just opinion. A study conducted by researchers at the University of Pennsylvania's Annenberg School for Communication suggests that longer tweets—280 rather than 140 characters—breed civility.

Professor Yphtach Lelkes and his team, writing in the *Journal of Communication*, said they analyzed tweets from before and after Twitter increased its tweet character limit to 280 in 2017. They concluded that the average quality of conversation improved.[13]

They defined quality as an ideal form of political debate, and evaluated tweets for clarity, polite language, justification of opinions, and the use of facts or links to more information. They also evaluated whether users exchanged ideas rather than simply shouting insults at each other. It seems that the increased tweet length let people explain themselves; they could be more deliberative, polite, and civil.

Professor Lelkes says his findings might not apply across all social media. Facebook isn't Twitter, he notes, and there are too many differences amongst various social media outlets. He's using a grant from Facebook to study how different aspects of technology lend themselves to different conversations and actions.

By the way, Cardi B's daughter is named "Kulture Kiari Cephus." That's six characters longer than "Bernie Sanders."

I DON'T SEE WHY YOU WOULDN'T READ ON

During a joint press conference between President Donald Trump and Russian President Vladimir Putin in July 2018, a question was raised about whether Mr. Trump thought Russia intervened or meddled in the American 2016 presidential election. Mr. Trump answered that he "didn't see why it would be Russia," but some in his camp later argued he meant to say "wouldn't."[14] Rather than getting into a hoo-ha over did he or didn't he mean what he said, I instead decided this issue could best be tackled from a grammatical standpoint in a conversation about contractions.

The character of Mr. Data on *Star Trek: The Next Generation*, an android played by actor Brent Spiner, did not use contractions when he spoke. This was a linguistic trick used by the writers of that television series to emphasize that Data was a machine, albeit a very lifelike one.

Star Trek's writers also had some fun with an alternative Data character, specifically his evil twin brother, Lore, (yes, there was an "evil Data") who did use contractions when he spoke. That was another linguistic trick to help viewers tell the two characters—both played by Mr. Spiner with the help of special effects—apart.

OK, a quick *mea culpa*. The writers occasionally slipped up and put a contraction or two in Mr. Data's dialogue. There's actually a blog charting Data's dialogue in all 176 episodes of the show—TheTrekBBS.com—which is probably a level of detail only die-hard fans of the *Star Trek* universe would appreciate.

That said, to address the elephant in the room, Mr. Data would have said "I do not see why it would not be Russia" while Lore would have said "I *don't* see why it *wouldn't* be Russia."

The use—or non-use—of contractions is understandable. They are a part of language and have been a part of the spoken word for well over 400 years. Today, they make us sound more conversational, and they probably shave a millisecond or two off the time it takes to write some sentences or phrases.

The earliest contractions are found in seventh century Old English. That's what everyone spoke when *Beowulf* was a best-seller ... or best-listen since, as I mentioned earlier, scholars suspect that epic story was first told around a campfire in the pre-flashlight-in-the-face time.

Some of the contractions used in Old English include:

- Nis for Neis / is not
- Naefde for ne haefde / did not have
- Naes for ne weaes / was not
- Nolde for ne wolde / would not (See what I just did there?)

One wonders if Beowulf would have said "Yfel wîtan forhwon yfel sîn Grendel's sweostor." (Translation: "I don't see why I wouldn't be Grendel's father.")

Old English faded away, but contractions certainly did not. Shakespeare *loved them*:

- Durst/dared
- Doth/do or does
- Dar'st/dare
- Ere/before
- Fare you well/good-bye
- Ha'/have
- Hast/have
- Prithee/I pray thee or I ask thee
- Sham'st/are ashamed
- Whit/a bit or piece
- Whe'er/whenever

Since the character of Mr. Data was highly cerebral, it comes as no surprise that academic writing shuns the use of contractions. A blog for the *American Psychological Association Publication Manual*, one of the cornerstone reference guides for scholarly scribes, gives a Miss Thistlebottom "tsk tsk" to the use of contractions, cautioning, "Contractions are a part of informal writing. Thus, avoid contractions in scholarly writing."[15]

As with any part of our language, there are exceptions—reproductions of dialect and quotations, an academic paper specifically about contractions, and use of idioms ("don't count your chickens before they hatch"), to name a few.

AND LASTLY
A presentation by my colleague Mike Deas, "The Art of Logic in Language," pointed to disconnects we commit when communicating, such as two signs at a motor vehicle inspection station. The first one tells car drivers to turn off their radios, yet the second sign says, "For More Information Tune to 107.5 on your Radio." His presentation reminded me of one of my favorite pet peeves: the sign in a restaurant bathroom that reads, "Employees Must Wash Hands." Trust me, I have stood in that damn bathroom and no employee shows up to wash my hands. (Think about that one.)

Let's write carefully out there, people.

5

the business of writing

It was a classic cringeworthy moment. It was 1988, and I was
interviewing candidates for an assistant account executive job
at the public relations agency where I worked. And yes, cringeworthy was a word in 1988. *Merriam-Webster* says so.[1]

The eager young man interviewing for the job proudly said
he could "write up a storm," then added, somewhat bashfully,
"except for the grammar part."

Well, that was a first. This man admitted something I never
admitted to in all the job interviews I had endured. His honesty
was refreshing.

I did not hire him. But his honesty was nevertheless
refreshing.

Finding a good writer can be a challenge. I guess it's easier to separate the wheat from the chaff when the candidate admits they cannot do the job. If the job requires one to write clearly, then you either can or you cannot.

A common tactic used by employers to identify good writers is administering a writing test, which only measures one's knowledge of English grammar and spelling. The eager beaver I interviewed would have, by his own admission, crashed and burned on such a test. (I would have, too.) Since he said he could "write up a storm," he might have been able to make thunderclouds form as he turned a phrase. How could I tell? How, indeed, do you measure creativity in someone's writing?

The Fargus Writing Test is my answer, and I wish I had known about it in 1988. I came across it while reading through some public relations professional journals. For years, I have looked for the genius who created it because I really want to give credit to that person. If you're out there, kudos! And please don't sue me for using it here. I really tried to find you.

By the way, this is one of the few columns that appeared both in the original print version of AFWAW that was around in the 1990s and in the email version when it was resurrected in 2017. I shared it both times because the feedback I receive is always positive. It underscores that there is an audience who cares about the written word. Plus, there are readers who took the test and sent me their work! One reader, back in the 1990s, called me after taking the test and shared what he did to ask if he passed. (Postscript: he did.)

For fun: send me your work if you decide to take the test. I grade on a curve (josephdiorio56@gmail.com).

QUIZ: A GOOD WRITER WON'T EVEN HAVE TO TAKE THIS TEST

Background:

Fred Fargus, CEO of the Fargus Corporation, traveled to East Falls to speak with city officials and employees at the Fargus Corp.'s new factory. The factory is still under construction. The city of East Falls gave Fargus a lot of tax incentives to get the company to move its new factory to their town. So far, however, the factory construction is behind schedule, and the number of people hired is far smaller than initial projections.

Fargus traveled to East Falls in the company Learjet. He was accompanied by Miss Frannie Chippie, his "secretary" who is rumored to soon become his third wife.

When the company Learjet finished taxiing and the steps were rolled up to the doorway, Fargus emerged, martini in hand, and promptly tripped and fell down the stairs. Miss Chippie, who was standing right behind Fargus, appeared more interested in taking a selfie with the jet in the background than the well-being of her employer/possible fiancé.

While on the ground ... well, once he was *standing,* Fargus made some vague promises to get the project back on budget and on schedule.

Assignment:

Write the headline and the first paragraph of a story from the perspective of:

- The Fargus Company director of public relations.
- *The Wall Street Journal's* business beat reporter who has been covering Fargus for several years.

- *The East Falls Times'* beat reporter.
- The local TV news anchor.
- The East Falls' daily newspaper humor columnist.

Good writers will have fun with this assignment. But you can easily tell who is going to ace this test before they write a single word because the good writers all do the same thing as they read the instructions.

They smile.

POWER OF THE SPOKEN WORD

Peggy Noonan and I have a lot in common. We're both from the Northeastern United States. We are both writers. And we were both speechwriters for presidents.

Now, Noonan established herself as the primary speechwriter for President Ronald Reagan and, later, President George H.W. Bush. Me? I was the speechwriter for the president of IBM's primary U.S. marketing operation. Hey, that operation was responsible for a couple billion dollars of revenue every year. I also freelanced a number of speeches for speakers I never met and, therefore, have no idea if they used a word of what I wrote. But I *did* write the speeches.

Noonan and I also had the joy of writing for someone who was an exceptionally good speaker. Ronald Reagan was called "The Great Communicator" for a reason. He knew the power of the spoken word. Earlier in this book, I referenced Reagan's speech delivered on the day that the Space Shuttle Challenger exploded shortly after liftoff. That wasn't his only great oration. At his first inauguration, he recalled the then relatively unknown story of a World War I soldier named Martin Treptow who had left his barber shop in Cherokee, Iowa to fight in the war, writing home to friends that America must win this war, and that he will sacrifice all to achieve that goal.

> "The crisis we are facing today does not require of us the kind of sacrifice that Martin Treptow and so many thousands of others were called upon to make. It does require, however, our best effort, and our willingness to believe in ourselves and to believe in our capacity to perform great deeds; to believe that together, with God's help, we can and will resolve the problems which now confront us. And, after all, why shouldn't we believe that? We are Americans."[2]

Man, that's some powerful speech making.

(Full disclosure, Noonan most likely didn't write that speech since she came on board later in 1981. Still, good writing is as good writing does.)

My guy, a gentleman named Mike Quinlan (and a former Navy pilot), was not Ronald Reagan, but he understood the power of the spoken word. One year, during an all-hands sales conference in New York City, Mike was scheduled to deliver a speech about the sales incentive program, which is how IBM sales professionals are paid. By any measure, the sales incentive program at IBM was a complex set of rules, regulations, guidelines, and benchmarks that some argued was designed just to confound the salesmen and keep them from making too much money. Mike knew IBM was working hard on simplifying the incentive program, but the work to revamp the program was not completely done. What *was done* was the removal of a lot of the bureaucratic red tape. So, near the outset of his speech on the program, he said,

"We have simplified the rules. We did away with them altogether." For added effect he tossed aside some sheets of paper. As they say in show business, the audience went wild.

But there is a catch. A good speech is hard to deliver and equally hard to write. Most people who need to stand before an audience don't know what they want to say, or they get wrapped up in coming up with a PowerPoint presentation to accompany them. (When I worked for IBM the executives who had to make speeches demanded PowerPoints—we called them slides and/or foils back then—and emphasized they needed lots of "big animal pictures" for their speeches, meaning they needed images on a screen to not only get their point across but also to help them feel comfortable.)

Some of the best speeches are TedX talks. A good friend, Lily Clayton Hansen, delivered a wonderful TedX talk about how meeting with and talking to new people was her personal therapy.[3] Her talk was titled "Talking to strangers is my superpower." Like all TedX talks, it was excellent. But this presentation involved weeks and weeks of preparation, rehearsal, rewrites, tweaks, even meetings with acting coaches … all to make it seem like she was delivering the talk off the cuff … or not prepared at all.

Public speaking is hard. But there are tools and techniques to make it easier.

THE 10/20/30 RULE FOR SPEECHES AND PRESENTATION

Mike Quinlan was not the only IBM executive who I wrote speeches for. I was assigned to support several executives for speechwriting. Mike, as I said, was very good. There were others who, well, I will leave it that they were otherwise good at their jobs.

Rather than using names, I'll just refer to Mike and the other fellows as the "good" speaker and the "others."

The good speaker rarely used slides and kept his talks to 20 minutes or less. The others? I once had to create a slide to *explain* a previous slide in one of their presentations. And one routinely needed at least 10 minutes just to introduce themself.

Point made. I'm not here to kick anyone when they're down … or just not in the room. Public speaking is hard. And it is only getting harder in a social media world. Apple recently said it limits executives to *ten minutes* for a speech because neuroscience proves that our brains get bored and stop listening after that amount of time. I once wrote a speech for the good speaker at IBM that was loaded with data—sales figures, revenue projects, arithmetic that would make Pythagoras proud.

When it came time for the speech to be delivered, I staked out a spot in the back of the auditorium to listen. Sitting next to me was an IBM executive who was taking copious notes as the speaker delivered number after number and presented slide after slide.

Unfortunately, the speech I wrote was 20 minutes long and since the fellow taking notes was writing as he was listening, he wound up writing down every number incorrectly. This was all the more amazing since there were PowerPoint slides with the correct numbers on them.

That taught me that PowerPoint slides alone don't make a good speech. Google's Sundar Pichai delivered a speech with zero bullet points. He understood that stories are best told with pictures, not text on a screen. Text on a screen means the audience must either listen to you or read. It's hard to do both.

Some speechwriters have sound advice on making good presentations in today's social media world.

"I follow the '10/20/30' rule. Ten slides to present in 20 minutes and nothing smaller than 30-point type on the slides," says Thomas Mattia, a public relations professional who ran communications for Coca Cola, Yale University, Electronic Data Systems, and Ford Motor Company. "You have to make your points as convincing as possible in the shortest amount of time." He teaches a storytelling class at Rutgers University and has students follow the 10/20/30 rule.

The message and good writing are the primary concerns for veteran speechwriters. "A picture may be worth 1,000 words, but a picture of 1,000 words is worthless," notes Boe Workman, director of CEO Communications for AARP. Workman is firm in his belief that the slide is not the speech.

Liz DeCastro, executive director of marketing communications and events for the National Council on Compensation Insurance (NCCI), says she has a team working on developing images that support rather than repeat a speaker's message.

"I once sat in on a presentation on a very technical subject," DeCastro says. "The speaker used no notes, and the images supported—not repeated—what he said. I always try to take that approach myself."

Workman said the length of a speech is secondary to the quality of writing. "I don't buy that a 10-minute speech is hard to do," he says. "People can't listen to a five-minute speech if it's not written well. If well written, then the audience will be mesmerized by it."

ANYBODY HAVE SOUND BITE SOFTWARE?

Actor Allison Janney delivered a humorous sound bite when she accepted her 2018 Oscar for Best Supporting Actress in the movie

I, Tonya. At the outset of her acceptance speech, she said, "I did it all myself." After the audience laughter died down, she went on to thank the litany of people who she couldn't have done it without. Specifically, she said of everyone who helped her, "You represent everything that is good and right and human."[4]

Janney's initial comment became one of the quote-worthy and tweet-worthy moments of the night. She actually delivered *two* very good sound bites. In case you are wondering (I was), a sound bite is defined by *Merriam-Webster* as "a brief recorded statement from a public official or celebrity."[5] Janney's tongue-in-cheek comment, "I did it all myself," was the perfect sound bite.

While I was delighted for the positive impact of Janney's one-liner, I also cringed at the memory of my speech writing days when I'd be asked to insert some good sound bites into the script I was writing. That request always grated on me because you can't just write a sound bite.

But can you? The short answer is "it depends." The longer answer is that short messages have become an integral part of everyone's communication diet.

"There were more than a few times when my phone would ring, and my boss would say, 'Lynn get over here. We need something pithy." says Lynn McCloud Dorfman who wrote for executives with USAirways (now American Airlines), the Federal Aviation Administration, and the National Transportation Safety Board. "At first I didn't even know what 'pithy' meant!"

Short, compact, and—yes—sometimes "pithy" messages are an integral part of communication today, especially since so much of our national discourse takes place over social media. A speech writer today looks to capture messages in increasingly short and concise manners.

Nathan Osburn, who wrote speeches for the head of the U.S. Department of Commerce, wrote the line with former U.S. Commerce Secretary Penny Pritzker: "America is open for business."[6] He says he didn't always write memorable sound bites.

In an interview, Osburn explains that speech writers today may have to think more about sound bites than ever before. The executive message you are working on—whether it is for investors, parents and graduates at commencement, or a sales meeting—may be echoed and amplified through numerous outlets. "You have to work with the public relations team and whoever is running social media because the speech will go into a press release, it will be excerpted by your own organization on Twitter, and it may be captured and shared on YouTube," he says.

Osburn also notes, "You're working in a 21st century communications shop…The spoken word is delivered in a lot of different ways. It has to be able to cut through the clutter."

During her interview, Dorfman elaborates, "David McCullough once said good writing is good thinking." When Peggy Noonan (the aforementioned speechwriter for Ronald Reagan) was interviewed before President Obama's first inauguration, she was asked if Obama's speech would have any memorable lines. I loved her answer, which was "I hope not. I hope they all are thinking."

That's not to say Dorfman did not write any memorable sound bites throughout her career. She was penning speeches for the NTSB when the agency was recommending a ban on texting while driving and wrote the line: "No call, no text, no update is worth a human life."

The nuts and bolts of a good speech boils down to good research and preparation. Dorfman is a proponent of heavily researching the subject, the audience, and the speaker's expertise; then marrying the three into a message. "The research and prep work you do for a speech is what's under the tip of the iceberg," she says.

She compares a good speech to good directions on Google maps. "It takes you by the hand and presents facts in a logical progression." That logic was put to work when she wrote a speech for the head of the Federal Aviation Administration, who was talking to airline lobbying groups after 9/11. The speech presented a history of aviation security, weaving a storyline from its early days to the post-9/11 world. "We were entering a new world of aviation security; the message was well-received," Dorfman says.

Osburn echoes agreement in his comments. "The speeches I remember best are those with the strongest possible flow to them, the ones that weaved a story throughout and takes the audience on a journey of what the speaker believes," he says.

In that case, one isn't really doing it alone. Allison Janney would agree.

SOUND BITE QUIZ

Here is a list of sound bites from memorable speeches. Can you match the sound bite in List A to the speaker in List B? (FYI, somebody won a $5 Starbucks gift card when I included a version of this in the newsletter. For this, you get the satisfaction of knowing you were right.)

List A—The Sound bites

A	"I don't want you to be hopeful. I want you to panic... and act as if the house was on fire."
B	"Hello gorgeous."
C	"Ich bin ein Berliner."
D	"Again, you can't connect the dots looking forward; you can only connect them looking backward."
E	"[Y]ou've got to ask yourself one question: 'Do I feel lucky?'"
F	"A lot of times, we censor ourselves before the censor even gets there."
G	"We were highly resolve that the dead shall not have died in vain."

List B—Who said it?

1	Barbara Streisand
2	Greta Thunberg
3	President John F. Kennedy
4	President Abraham Lincoln
5	Clint Eastwood
6	Spike Lee
7	Steve Jobs

WHEN IN DOUBT, ASK THE GREEK PHILOSOPHERS

Garry Wills, in his Pulitzer Prize winning book, *Lincoln at Gettysburg: The Words That Remade America*, writes how the Greek Athenians sorted out their emotions through their oratory.[14] Their feelings and observations can be broken down into some basic components, which I offer my take on here.

Not every speechwriter thinks in terms of the polarities that follow, but aspects of them creep into every speech we write, deliver, and hear. In fact, I would go so far as to propose these aspects are guidelines for speechwriters to use when composing their oration.

(ANSWER KEY: 1B[7], 2A[8], 3C[9], 4G[10], 5E[11], 6F[12], 7D[13])

1.   **The one/the many**. This theme holds true from great speeches like the Gettysburg Address: "The world will little note, nor long remember what we say here, but it can never forget what they did here." Or how about how that time Mr. Spock explained his suicidal actions in *Star Trek II: The Wrath of Kahn*, telling Captain Kirk before dying, "The needs of the many outweigh the needs of the one."[15]

2.   **Lightness and darkness**. President Bill Clinton at his first inauguration declared, "There is nothing wrong with America that cannot be cured by what is right with America."[16] In the early days of the COVID-19 pandemic, Queen Elizabeth II addressed the British nation, the world, saying "If we remain united and resolute, then we will overcome it … Better days will return: we will be with our friends again; we will be with our families again; we will meet again."[17]

3.   **Mortal and immortal**. Life is short, but what soldiers accomplish on the battlefield will live on forever. On the 40th anniversary of the Allied invasion of Normandy, President Ronald Reagan stood before the surviving U.S. Army Rangers who had climbed the hills to take out Nazi artillery, and said to a grateful crowd, "These are the boys of Pointe du Hoc. These are the men who took the cliffs. These are the champions who helped free a continent. These are the heroes who helped end a war."[18]

4.   **Us and others**. The Athenians believed they were uniquely positioned in the world. This can also be interpreted as "we are ready and able to do what we know is right." One of Winston Churchill's three speeches to the House of Parliament in the early days of World War II included this moving passage:

"But if we fail, then the whole world, including the United States, including all that we have known and cared for, will sink into the abyss of a new dark age made more sinister, and perhaps more protracted, by the lights of perverted science. Let us therefore brace ourselves to our duties, and so bear ourselves, that if the British Empire and its Commonwealth last for a thousand years, men will say, 'This was their finest hour.'"[19]

5.   **Words and deeds**. An effort by the hero is remembered not only if successful—historians write of Pickett's Charge during the Battle of Gettysburg, or the Charge of the Light Brigade. Those guys lost. But they believed to the core in what they were doing. Sheryl Sandberg, addressing graduates at the University of California, Berkeley in 2016, said,

"It's the hard days—the days that challenge you to your very core—that determine who you are. You will be defined not just by what you achieve, but how you survive. When the challenges come, I hope you remember that anchored deep within you is the ability to learn and grow. You are not born with a fixed amount of resilience. Like a muscle, you can build it up, draw on it when you need it."[20]

6.   **Teachers and taught**. Experiences and knowledge are always passed down. "It's evolution, man. Eventually the student becomes the teacher."—Big Sean.[21] (Yeah, there are other examples. But I don't get to quote a rapper very often.)

7.   **Age and youth**. Age is expected to beget both knowledge and experience. When he spoke to graduates at Stanford University, Apple founder Steve Jobs encouraged graduates to find their unique path. He discussed his own personal and professional journey and the lessons he learned along the way. He also cited

the final edition of *The Whole Earth Catalog*, which contains the words: Stay Hungry. Stay Foolish. "I have always wished that for myself," Jobs said. "And now, as you graduate to begin anew, I wish that for you."[22]

8. **Male and female**. Pericles often addressed parents and sons with this analogy, but the idea is the juxtaposition between a pair—be that a parent and child, enemies and allies, opposite political parties. The message is the strengths and uniqueness the combined two present. Poet Amanda Gorman captured this spirit during her poem, "Together We Rise," delivered during President Joseph R. Biden's inauguration. She wrote, "Somehow we do it. Somehow we weathered and witnessed a nation that isn't broken, but simply unfinished. We, the successors of a country and a time where a skinny Black girl descended from slaves and raised by a single mother can dream of becoming president, only to find herself reciting for one."[23]

9. **Choice and determination**. We make choices on behalf of others.

"We dare not forget today that we are the heirs of that first revolution. Let the word go forth from this time and place, to friend and foe alike, that the torch has been passed to a new generation of Americans—born in this century, tempered by war, disciplined by a hard and bitter peace, proud of our ancient heritage—and unwilling to witness or permit the slow undoing of those human rights to which this Nation has always been committed."—John F. Kennedy at his inauguration, January 20, 1961.[24]

10. **Past and present**. Pericles said we draw strength from the past when we chart our future. Speaking before fans on Lou Gehrig Day at Yankee Stadium during his battle with amyotrophic lateral sclerosis, Lou Gehrig remarked, "I've had a tough break, but today I consider myself the luckiest man on the face of the earth."[25]

TO RULE OR NOT TO RULE

Writer and educator Mark Edwards keeps a long list of writing tips, and there is a tinge of irony to them.

"Rule #683: Don't ever write it down—plot, story, sentence—unless it's PERFECT IN YOUR MIND."

"Rule #677: Your first draft is FANTASTIC. Don't let anyone tell you otherwise." (This, of course, is contrary to advice attributed to Ernest Hemingway, "The first draft of anything is shit.")

"Rule #676: Each day open the thesaurus and find cool new words—and just jam them into whatever you're working on."

OK, let me rephrase that. His advice is loaded with irony. Edwards is a communications and media studies adjunct instructor at Sacred Heart University in Fairfield, Connecticut, and he has encountered his share of would-be Hemingways. His writing tips appear on his Facebook page.

His advice is a stress relief tool and a reminder to remain vigilant when writing something you want someone else to read.

Edwards also shares a personal story of when a writer he considered a mentor sat him down and said, "All right, you are good enough where I can tell you how bad your writing is without making you stop writing." Harsh? Perhaps. But sometimes harsh is necessary.

"There's a kind of narcissism that ties into people's writing where it's all about them rather than, God forbid, writing three sentences in a row that are compelling," Edwards says.

Are there over 600 writing tips that Edwards has written down somewhere? "In my mind, perhaps yes," Edwards says. Part of the reason he numbered the pieces of advice so randomly, he explains, is the nature of the internet. "When online, you may always feel you are suddenly coming in on the middle of an ongoing [conversation]." His random numbering is just his way of continuing the idea of an ongoing conversation.

DULL WRITING = BAD MARKETING

Dull writing, in an age when we seem to spend less and less time looking at the written word, is the proverbial kiss of death for marketing communication professionals trying to carve out a niche for their companies or clients.

Over a decade ago, writer Nicholas Carr asked, "Is Google making us stupid?" in a 2008 *The Atlantic* article.

"Immersing myself in a book or a lengthy article used to be easy," he wrote.

> "My mind would get caught up in the narrative or the turns of the argument, and I'd spend hours strolling through long stretches of prose. That's rarely the case anymore. Now my concentration often starts to drift after two or three pages. I get fidgety, lose the thread, begin looking for something else to do. I feel as if I'm always dragging my wayward brain back to the text. The deep reading that used to come naturally has become a struggle." He discussed the scan and graze nature of reading in the age of instant information. "[The] Net seems to be … chipping away at my capacity for concentration and contemplation."[26]

In the ensuing years, social media seems to have done to prose what Google may have done to reading. The demand for quick and up-to-the-nanosecond communication is leaving good writing in its wake. A quick scan of my news feeds on Twitter and LinkedIn shows the text in each post possesses the same banal monotony.

- "We are so proud …"
- "Today I had the chance to …"
- "This is super interesting …"
- "Humbled by my introduction to …"
- "Excited to announce …"

People, people, please stop! We can do better.

OK, so writing and grammar are ever-evolving. Fans of William Safire's "On Language" columns in the Sunday edition of *The New York Times* understand this. Also, there is a lot of pressure to produce content. Jayson DeMers wrote in a 2014 *Forbes* article titled, "Is bad grammar killing your brand?" that "The growth of the internet means that everyone is publishing more content than ever … the sheer volume of social media posts, articles, blog posts, images, videos, and more means that there's that much more potential for error."[27]

We need good writing when people spend less time reading. Is there a solution? Yep. "Omit needless words" advises *The Elements of Style*.[28] Each of those introductory lines cited above can and should be axed. We know you are proud, excited, and humbled. Tell us WHY you are that way.

Ted Sorensen, whom I had the privilege of meeting in 2009, gave me the same advice but with more style than I can muster.

I'll shorten his advice since you may be reading this online … or this passage found its way into a Google search result. (Yes, that was sarcastic.)

He said a salesman was setting up shop to sell seafood. His first pass at a sign: "Fresh Seafood, Fish for Sale." Well, the salesman thought, who would sell stale fish? He shortened the sign to "Seafood, Fish for Sale." Heck, fish *are* seafood, so the word "fish" was dropped. But if I'm selling seafood in a store why say it's for sale? The final sign outside his store read, simply, "Seafood."

And, by the way, I'm confident he was proud, excited, and humbled by the chance to open his store.

THE BEST AND THE BRIGHTEST DIDN'T WRITE THE MANUAL

Here's a corporate urban legend about computer manuals.

I had to read a lot when I started my job at IBM in 1982. I was responsible for publicizing how customers in the Southeastern U.S. used IBM products, but first, I had to get up-to-speed on computers and computer-industry news. Yes, I said "computers." This was the early 80s and the word "laptop" had not been coined. No one called them PCs, and virtually no one was using the internet.

So, I read news magazines, *The New York Times, The Wall Street Journal, Computer Week,* and dozens of other trade magazines.

I also read IBM user manuals about products called the System/360 mainframe, the System/36 mid-size computer, and this quirky product no one at IBM wanted to sell called the IBM Personal Computer. I would spend days reading user manuals. When I finished, I always had the following revelation: I didn't know anything more about IBM computers than I did before I started.

Each book began with the following line (these aren't the exact words, but they're close): "Before reading this manual, refer to technical journal XXXXXXXX." And once I found this missing manual, IT told me to find yet *another* manual for further reference.

I never found "manual zero," but I did learn why IBM user manuals were so poorly written.

Back in the 1980s, IBM didn't fire people. "Full employment" was the company line. If you were hired by IBM, then you had a job for life.

But what if you were bad at your job? No problem. IBM's human resources folks would have you reassigned to a different job. And if you were bad at that new job, you would be reassigned yet again. This process would continue indefinitely. Well, almost indefinitely. Now for the corporate urban legend.

Eventually more than a few employees were found to be so bad at everything that the folks in human resources were left flummoxed as to where to assign them. Were those bad employees fired?

Nope. They were tasked with writing user manuals.

That's right. Legend has it that the least talented people—the ones who couldn't do any other job well—were responsible for writing user manuals explaining how to use IBM products.

The story I just shared is, as I say, just a legend. Still, I often wondered who would use IBM user manuals, and I think the answer is virtually no one. Not even people who work for IBM.

I say that with confidence based on personal experience. (What follows is *not* an urban legend.)

By 1991, I had left IBM and started working as a freelance writer. My wife still worked for IBM; she was a Systems Engineer responsible for helping customers set up their computers. We used her employee discount to buy an IBM Personal Computer for my business. When the PC arrived, she ripped open the box and started setting up the PC. Yes, you had to set up a new PC: load software, plug the monitor in to the processor, and so on. Bear in mind, however, that my wife had never set up a PC before. Remember I said IBM sales professionals didn't like selling PCs. The commissions were too small.

While setting up the PC, she had tossed aside the manual. I picked it up, held it out toward her, and said, "Don't you want to look at this?"

She stopped long enough to look at what I was holding and said, "Oh, screw that!"

This essentially sums up the value of another written product that shows up in corporate offices: the editorial style guide.

EDITORIAL STYLE GUIDES—A PROJECT WE NEVER GET TO

I am frequently asked about creating an internal editorial style guide. It's a request that frequently makes me cringe.

My employer once implemented an internal editorial style guide. It had detailed rules and standards for the written word, right down to how a facsimile cover sheet should be formatted. This should tell you two things: (1) Yes, I am talking about a fax machine; this was a long time ago, and (2) How one formats a fax cover sheet really isn't an editorial judgment; alas, the bureaucracy must be cultivated before it is served.

A co-worker who took pride in his rebellious streak announced that, no matter what, he would NOT use the specified format for fax cover sheets. "It's small-minded rule-making," he proclaimed. (Well, page 15 of *The Elements of Style*, which says "choose a suitable design and hold to it," differs with his proclamation.[29] But I digress.)

I don't know if Mr. Rebel followed through on his promise to be a formatting outlier. It really wasn't important enough to check. And therein lies one of the problems with in-house editorial style guides. They are created and go into someone's desk drawer or computer folder. Another more important problem, though, is since a reference tool like *Strunk and White* succinctly addresses one of the topics covered in an internal style guide (consistency of format), is the creation of said style guide necessary?

If you are ever tasked with creating an in-house editorial and/or writing style guide for your business, and the number of you who have been asked are legion, please heed my advice:

1. Don't.
2. If you must, then read on.

I suspect every company out there has an in-house rebel who, no matter what, isn't going to follow the rules. And the grammar police ("To Serve and Correct") don't have universal enforcement jurisdiction.

Moreover, *The Chicago Manual of Style* is nearly 1,000 pages chock-full of writing style advice for virtually everybody. Pair that with *Strunk and White* (Look through your desk. I'm betting there's a copy in there somewhere.), and you have the crux of an internal editorial style guide. And I will further bet that your in-house rebel (come on, we all have one) will be happy to follow *those* style guides.

Yes, there are some things standard guides like *Chicago, Strunk and White*, and the *Associated Press Stylebook* don't cover, like how your company name is spelled (using "and" rather than

"&," for example), how the company logo should look, where it should and shouldn't appear, what colors comprise the company logo, and what typeface is used on the company website and in printed materials. Those are design questions that are important in helping differentiate a company. The editorial questions, however, are covered in *Chicago, Strunk & White,* and *AP.*

What about state abbreviations, you ask? *Chicago* section 15.29 instructs: spell out and use the two-letter abbreviation only when it is followed by the ZIP code. Nearby section 15.31 explains where punctuation goes in a city and state construction.

When using a computer keyboard, are you using the "shift" key or the "Shift" key? *Chicago* section 7.77 says to capitalize.

Got something you say is off topic, like bias free language? Sections 5.203 through 5.206 suggest, "Language that is either sexist or suggestive of other conscious or subconscious prejudices … distracts and may even offend readers."

I could go on with a war of attrition over "does it or doesn't it" cover your unique needs, but let me instead offer a compromise.[30]

The Chicago Manual of Style, The Elements of Style, and throw in *The Associated Press Stylebook* are available through Amazon for about $70. Divide the amount of time you may spend creating an internal style guide by what you earn. I'm willing to bet it's more than $70. Then, before you start building your style guide, suggest to the boss that you at least try buying the books for a small number of staff members and see if that suffices. Many years ago, IBM gave its employees in corporate communications their own copy of the *AP Stylebook.* It certainly was more effective than re-creating the wheel.

Let's write carefully out there, people.

6

phraseology follies

Readers of the late William Safire's "On Language" column in *The New York Times Sunday Magazine* remember the "Squad Squad"; readers who would submit examples of redundant language.

The work of the Squad Squad came to mind when a reader of AFWAW pointed out an example where a federal grand jury investigation was described as a "Rigged Witch Hunt."

Merriam-Websters' secondary definition of "rigged" is fixed in place, as a sail on a boat.[1] The *Urban Dictionary* defines the term as an unfair advantage given to someone. Said dictionary also defines "witch hunt" as a targeted attack against one person, for reasons that are not necessarily tangible.[2] Taken together, then, a "Rigged Witch Hunt" does seem to qualify as redundant.

I'm sure there was no collusion in that grammatical construction.

Here's another item from the Squad Squad files. In January 2019, the White House said the State of the Union speech should be delivered "on time and on schedule."

Here is another pet peeve of mine. The White House is a big, old building. It didn't say anything. However, one late night TV host mined that line for humor to say the "on time and on schedule" is redundant. Well, not exactly.

The *Oxford English Dictionary* defines on time as being "punctual" or "in good time."[3] A third definition offered *is* "on schedule," which Oxford also defines as "on time, as planned or expected."

Our language is rife with homonyms (words with the same spelling and pronunciation but have different meanings), homophones (words with the same pronunciation but different spelling and meanings), and homographs (words spelled the same but have different pronunciations and meanings); so it isn't surprising that there could be multiple combinations of words that mean either the same thing or slightly different things. This time around I had to side with the talking building and say there was no redundancy.

KICKING OUR APOLOGIES UP A NOTCH

"Joseph, you apologize to Thomas *like you mean it.*" It's an admonishment I vividly recall some 50-plus years after my fourth-grade teacher directed me to express my regrets for punching a classmate. I had already muttered, "I'm sorry," but that wasn't cutting it with Mrs. Barachini. I dug an adverb out of my vocabulary, saying "I'm *really* sorry, Thomas" to get myself out of a one-way ticket to the principal's office.

(Postscript—I wasn't sorry. Thomas was a jerk, and he deserved that knuckle sandwich.)

My postscript is the rub—"rub" being a phrase first used by Shakespeare in *Hamlet*. My point is that a stack of adjectives or adverbs are often used to strengthen the sincerity of an apology.

Consider that there was a year where, within a few weeks of each other, several public officials were caught with their hands in the racist action cookie jar—see Virginia Governor Ralph Northam and Tennessee Governor Bill Lee for details, maybe with a side of Virginia Attorney General Mark Herring—and all of them cracked open the nearest thesaurus to make sure everyone knows they're really, really sorry. Northam, whose college yearbook contains what may or may not be a photograph of him wearing either a Klu Klux Klan hooded sheet or dressed in blackface as Michael Jackson, said he is "deeply sorry," while also saying he isn't sure either person in the photograph is him. (Thennnnnn how did the photo end up on your page in the yearbook, Ralph? Curiouser and curiouser, said Alice as she looked through the looking glass.) Northam expressed his regrets in a press release and through a news conference, emphasizing that he was very sorry.[4]

Meanwhile, in Tennessee, Governor Bill Lee's college yearbook contains a photo of the then young Tennessee governor decked out in a Confederate officer's uniform (gray *is* his color), and he said he regrets his actions and any distress they may have caused people.[5] Lastly, and not to be outdone, Virginia Attorney General Mark Herring played the "cut it off at the pass" card and said someone somewhere has a photo of him in blackface and that he was very, very sorry about that.[6] (Was there a market glut of black shoe polish back in the early 1980s?). He added he deeply, deeply regrets his decision. Herring's apology is especially surprising because no one ever produced said photograph. Makes one wonder how bad the real photo must be.

Using an adjective to modify a noun—as in saying "I'm really sorry, Thomas."—is a grammatical practice that has roots in Latin; it is an *adjectīvum* or additional noun. The use of said modifiers by politicians and one hot-headed fourth grader is described as *predictive* usage; said adjectives modify and—basically—strengthen the noun. The use of the double adverb by Herring may have changed the second "deeply" into an adjective, but let's not go down that rabbit hole. (The term "rabbit hole" comes from Lewis Carroll's *Alice in Wonderland*. Stop Googling it.[7]) An adverb's function is to limit or extend the significance of a verb. Its Latin roots come from *adverbium*, literally "that which is added to a verb."

How effective adverbs and adjectives are at enhancing the sincerity of one's regret is left to the recipient of the act. Mrs. Barachini believed me. Thomas, meanwhile, punched me in the back of the head the next day when no one was looking.

ILLEGAL PROCEDURES ON APOLOGIES

And speaking of apologies, Myles Garrett is a defensive lineman for the Cleveland Browns of the National Football League (NFL) who made dubious news on November 14, 2019 when, during a game, he ripped the helmet off the head of Pittsburgh Steelers quarterback Mason Rudolph and hit Rudolph in the head with said helmet.

Garrett received a hefty fine and a long suspension from the NFL for his action. He also said "I want to apologize" for the incident.[8] Not to kick a man when he's down—which is a 15-yard personal foul penalty in the NFL—but is that "Jeopardy" music I hear or did Garrett actually mean to just say, "I apologize?"

OUR AMAZING AND ABSORBENT LANGUAGE

Each summer the National Football League season appears on the horizon when 32 NFL teams commence their OTAs.

Wait, *what?*

In football, OTA means "Organized Team Activities," but you must search through sports pages to find OTA spelled out. (Kudos to those who help the football-impaired among us. This includes Cory Curtis, the sports director for Nashville's ABC affiliate, WKRN, who always begins with "Organized Team Activities, or OTAs.")

OTA can stand for many things, including "online ticket agent," "over the air" if you are talking about mobile phones, and, curiously, "offer to adopt." But Google "OTA" and the football reference comes up first. How did professional football commandeer that term? It is because American English is a very absorbent language. Note that I said "Google 'OTA,'" meaning Google can be a noun and a verb nowadays. Our language takes its vocabulary from many outside influences.

"There is something about [English] that is open to absorbing new words, whether from other languages, slangs, or made-up terms," says John Timpane, a consultant for business writing, former college professor, and the former theater critic, books editor, and arts reporter for *The Philadelphia Inquirer.* "The neat thing about this is that there are no rules. Once a word is absorbed, it's absorbed," he said in a telephone interview.

During the interview, Timpane notes that Americans have

been absorbing brand-new words forever. *We* started referring to the country as "USA." *We* started saying "OK," rather than "all right." Even terminology absorbed from one source can morph into words used in another setting, Timpane says. The word *psych*, as in "psych someone out," meaning "to intimidate psychologically," was a shortened form of that longer word. Later, *psych*, when added to the end of a statement, came to mean "fooled ya," and also "not really."

Timpane offers examples of other words that were created by various novel means or changed their meanings with use, including:

- *To pitchfork*: "a verb created from the name of a tool, a noun that itself is a wonderful combination of a verb (*to pitch*) married to a noun (*fork*)," Timpane says, as in "I pitchforked hay over the wall."

- *To deconstruct*: originally a term from a sophisticated literary-critical examination of written language, with time broadened its meaning. Today, it's often used to mean things like "take apart" or "destroy [e.g., an argument]." One entertaining current synonym is "to shred [e.g., an argument or point]," which in turn has an unrelated meaning in music, "to excel" or "to exhibit incredible mastery of an instrument."

- *Coming up*: a term that is coming to replace the term "growing up" in some parts of the United States.

- *Back in the day*: a term that has come to replace "in the olden days."

- *Swipe left*: a slang term, taken from an action on smart phone apps; outside of that activity, it means "to reject [i.e., sexually] or avoid [someone]."

If you want to have some fun tracking the rise and fall of words over time, look up Google's Ngram viewer, which charts both the rise and fall of words in the English language. Beware, though. Like any technology, it has its detractors. WIRED magazine notes it is overly science-centric, and some terms (like AIDS) don't show up at all.

A FEW MISCELLANEOUS ITEMS FROM THE PHRASEOLOGY FOLLIES

An empty crowd—period

One faithful reader noted a bottom third on a network news report saying there was an "empty crowd" at the Denver Zoo. Sparse crowds were a facet of the COVID-19 pandemic, except when they aren't (See party at the Lake of the Ozarks; any college campus; or Sturgis, South Dakota). In the case of the Denver Zoo, the line "empty crowd" is open for debate.

A crowd can be small, thin, overflowing, rambunctious, quiet, unruly, the largest in history *period*, and on and on. But a crowd, by definition, cannot be empty. It is the venue where the crowd may be—the zoo, an arena, a sports stadium, the National Mall in Washington, D.C.—that can be empty, period.

Talking about a wall

A lengthy shutdown of the federal government occurred in late 2018, because Republicans and Democrats could not agree on the definition of the word "wall." This of course pertained to the border between the United States and Mexico, which was an ongoing political hot potato. House Speaker Nancy Pelosi told *The New York Times* that the shutdown boils down to one's definition of the word "wall."[9] Concrete, steel, and a beaded curtain were offered up as examples.

For whatever it's worth, *Merriam-Webster* defines "wall" as a continuous vertical brick or stone structure that encloses or divides an area of land.[10] That seems to exclude beaded curtains, but I'm sure the debate will continue. And that's enough with our talk about decorative border accoutrements.

I have waited with baited (bated?) breath to tell you this

April 23 is the birthday of William Shakespeare, the man who first committed to paper many of the phrases and words we use today. According to some estimates, Shakespeare is responsible for over 1,600 words; if he didn't invent them, he was surely among the first to commit new words to paper.[11] And nearly 500 years after his birth, we still get many of his words wrong. Jen Horner, marketing and communications manager for Scriptis, USA, wrote about some of them.

For example, in *The Merchant of Venice,* Shylock asks whether his customers should expect him to speak "with bated breath and whisp'ring humbleness." Notice it is "bated" rather than "baited."

"Bate," Horner explains, comes from "abate" or "abatre" in old French, which means to beat down or diminish. Shylock, in this passage, is asking if he should stifle himself and speak in a hushed tone.

"Nowadays we don't speak with bated breath—we wait with bated breath," Horner writes. "What's more, lots of us wait with "baited" breath. I suppose we are hoping the bait on our breath will attract the thing we want, like the cat who eats cheese then waits by the mouse-hole."

Here's another one. When the character Macduff (from

the play *Macbeth*) hears that his entire family was murdered, he shouts, "Did you say all? O hell-kite! All? What, all my pretty chickens and their dam, at one fell swoop?"

OK, so a "kite" is a bird of prey (think "Chicken Hawk" from the old *Looney Tunes* cartoons) so this metaphor is of a flying raptor attacking chickens. But "fell" is an older word here, meaning terrible or evil. It comes from the word "felony," Horner writes, or a crime of some sort or another. Since our modern meaning of "fell" is of a downward motion, saying "one fell swoop" has come to mean sudden, or all at once. What it no longer means is evil. Which is why we can pick up the kids from school, do the grocery shopping, and stop at the FedEx store all in one fell swoop nowadays. The Bard would approve.

Did it hurt less than a collision?

Carnival Cruise Lines is calling the December 20, 2019, giant fender bender at sea between two of its cruise ships in Cozumel, Mexico an "allision" because only one of the giant ships was moving at the time of the snafu. *Merriam-Webster* agrees, pointing out the word is used almost exclusively when one ship bumps into a stationary vessel.[12] As Johnny Depp's *Pirates of the Caribbean* character, Captain Jack Sparrow, would say, it's a nautical term.

Space, the grammatical frontier

March 2020 marked the 54th anniversary of the flight of Gemini 8, the 51st anniversary of Apollo 9, and April 2020 was the 50th anniversary of Apollo 13.

OK, fess up. Unless you are a science and space nerd (like me), you didn't know any of that, did you?

Quick recap for the non-nerds in the audience: The Gemini

space flights, and the early Apollo flights were essentially test runs for a moon landing. Gemini had its name because there were only two astronauts on board the space capsule, making it a logical match for its astronomy cousin. The Apollo flights got their name because someone at NASA liked the image of the Greek God Apollo riding his chariot across the sun.

Gemini 8 and Apollo 9 were test flights leading up to the Apollo 11 moon landing, which happened in July 1969. Apollo 13 was to be the third manned landing on the moon, but part of the spaceship exploded, and the mission was aborted (everyone survived). Apollo 13 was chronicled in a really good Tom Hanks movie. Oh and, by the way, Neil Armstrong, who was the first person to walk on the moon, was the commander of Gemini 8.

Dates in the history of space flight may sometimes get lost in history, but space terms stick around in our language. Although they are not always used correctly.

For the anniversaries of those springtime space milestones, and considering that prime star gazing begins in the spring, I touched base with Janet Ivey, President of Explore Mars and CEO of the popular "Janet's Planet" television science segments to straighten out some space terms that are frequently misused.

Dark Side of the Moon: Besides referring to a Pink Floyd album, there is a persistent misnomer that the moon has a completely dark side. Scientists refute that, pointing out that while the moon is "tidally locked," meaning the same side always faces the Earth, that one side isn't dark. It is farther than the side with the Sea of Tranquility on it, fueling the urban reference that something being on the far side of the moon is remarkably far away.

While I'm at it, calling it a "sea" is a misnomer as well, although the genesis of that name doesn't reside in NASA's lap. The name was coined in 1651 by Francesco Grimaldi and his bestie Giovanni Battista Riccioli as they were doing some lunar cartography. They needed a familiar term to describe the large, open areas of the moon, and a nautical term seemed to work best.[13]

Sidebar: Janet Ivey mentioned that a member of her team—a scientist and an attorney—suggested in an email to her (which she subsequently shared with me) that since I am sharing what the moon *is not* made of, then I should go on to say what it is made of. In his email, he launched into a lengthy discussion of what comprises moon dust and moon rocks. This individual's very good insights didn't make the newsletter (it obviously didn't make the book, either). I used artistic license as my reason to omit this lengthy description. Suffice it to say, this individual's input confirms that the moon is not made of cheese.

Anyhow, *Merriam-Webster* defines "sea" as a "great body of saltwater,"[14] and Neil Armstrong didn't find any saltwater when he visited. Which brings me to the next section:

Search for water: The common misconception is that scientists are looking for a place to take a quick dip. It's a little different in space. Not only can no one hear your scream in space, but out there water can be a solid, liquid, or gas, and it is in a lot of places—the poles of Mercury, Pluto, the clouds of Venus, and several moons of Jupiter and Saturn all have traces of frozen water. It really isn't a search for water as much as it is a categorization.

Weightlessness or zero-g: Gravity doesn't go away once you are in space. Gravity is pulling us all the time, albeit not very much at 17,000 miles above the Earth. Rather than being weightless, in space you are in a constant state of freefall. The proximity of the celestial body that is pulling you determines how fast you fall.

Twinkling stars: Yeah, it sounds romantic all right, but the proper term is 'astronomical scintillation,' referring to what we see in the night sky. The twinkling—excuse me, scintillation—is caused by the Earth's atmosphere, which is made up of different layers that have different temperatures, densities, and other variables that cause light coming from a star to bend and refract.

Falling or shooting star: To be blunt, there ain't no such thing. Stars burn out. Sometimes they explode. But the streaks of light we sometimes see in the night sky are caused by tiny bits of dust and rock called meteoroids that are falling into Earth's atmosphere and burning up. If any part of a meteoroid survives the fall and lands on Earth, it is called a meteorite.

Life: Yep, this one is confusing too. All of us are conditioned to think of life *as we know it.* But scientists looking into space think of life in purely agnostic terms, searching for biosignatures (according to *Merriam-Webster,* a biosignature is a chemical compound, isotope, or cellular component that indicates or suggests the presence of a biological process indicative of life[15]) rather than E.T. waving at us as the Hubble Telescope peers into space.

Fan reaction: Any time I write about science in the newsletter, the feedback is abundant. Here's one reaction from a rather verbose reader.

> Gravity is still pretty strong at 27,360 km (17,000 miles) from the Earth's surface. Look at the Moon, which is 384,400 km distant, and it's held in the Earth's grasp.
>
> As you said, it's the free fall that produces weightlessness. You're also weightless when you jump off a diving board a couple meters above the Earth, at least until you hit the water. To prove this point, jump off the diving board while standing on a bathroom scale—you'll see the needle return to zero. (I would have to make sure I cleanly jump off the scale. I "clock in" at around 240 pounds, so the scale would not appreciate me landing on it.)
>
> The International Space Station, the Gemini capsules, and other human-occupied orbital spacecraft, skim just over the Earth's atmosphere, only about 400-500 kilometers above the surface, or roughly the distance between Washington, D.C., and your favorite city, Bridgeport (my hometown), only up. This is a big misconception that many people have—that orbital craft are in deep space.

This reader concluded their notes with a bit of grammar: "OK, I know you're going to say that I'm wrong when I capitalize 'Earth' and 'Moon.' But let's not forget that we capitalize 'Jupiter.' I'll also capitalize 'Hell' and 'Heaven' for the same reason—you would capitalize 'Valhalla' and 'Elysian,' no? Imaginary places get capitalized, too. And, for those who think that Heaven is real, what's its orbital radius?"

I honest-to-goodness love getting this kind of feedback. It means people are reading the newsletter and thinking critically about it.

Let's boldly go and write carefully out there, people.

7

a few words about numbers

SOME BASICS ABOUT NUMBERS

OK, I'm going to open this chapter with a quiz. (Stop complaining, it isn't hard.)

Here is a list of some of my favorite movies. Please put them in alphabetical order:

42
War of the Worlds
Titanic
2012
Star Wars
Bang the Drum Slowly

Easy, right? You start with *Bang the Drum Slowly* then … what? Where do you put *42* and *2012*?

The answer is that when putting numbers in a list of individual entries, you should put them in alphabetical order. Therefore, *42* (or forty-two) comes next, followed by *Star War*s (Han shot first when he killed Greedo, by the way, not the other way around), *Titanic*, *2012*, and finally, *War of the Worlds*.

That's one of those fuzzy little rules about our language that understandably may not be a top-of-mind factoid.

Numbers often dull the shine on our fascination with language. Some rules are ignored, unknown, strictly followed, or not strictly followed. We should, says *The Chicago Manual of Style,* spell out all numbers from one through one hundred.[1] Really? How often do we write or read, "a forty-watt lightbulb?" Isn't it normally written as "a 40-watt lightbulb?" Or a "30-year fixed loan?" So that rule isn't cast in stone, is it? Some newspapers I worked for spelled out one through nine … although that may have been for the same reason we would use lowercase letters when writing "street," "boulevard," "avenue," etc. (That reason, by the way, was that there was usually a shortage of capital letters available to the lead type linotype operators. Necessity is sometimes the mother of a style guide.)

Chicago also advises us to be flexible in our writing. As I said, the newspapers I worked for wanted reporters to spell out words from one through nine, then use the Arabic numerals thereafter. *Chicago* notes that the line, "12 eggs, of which nine were freshly laid yesterday" looks awkward, not to mention painful, as anyone who has tried to remove freshly laid eggs from a nest when a protective chicken is nearby knows. The key is flexibility.

AN ONGOING PET PEEVE

Speaking of frivolous usage, one of my biggest grammatical pet peeves comes from TV news whenever there is a heat wave. Inevitably someone on camera will say, "It's *a hundred* and one degrees outside today."

OK, you have probably read this before and by people other than me, but I'll share it here again. "A hundred" is an expression of volume, not a specific number. If the temperature outside is 101, you DON'T say "a hundred in one." You say, "one hundred and one degrees." Got it?

Apparently not, judging from the TV news I see just about everywhere.

I must add that TV meteorologists, who ad lib a lot of their lines, are some of the best newscasters at maintaining good grammar during their delivery of the weather forecast. Occasionally, though, a mistake slips through ... like when the local meteorologist posted a selfie while standing atop a parking garage on her Instagram account. Her caption read, "Taking pictures on top of a parking *gauge*, (my italics) totally normal thing to do." I couldn't let that one pass, so I wrote a reply on her Instagram asking, "Did you mean 'on top of a parking GARAGE'?"

"Fixed it, LOL. Also, overreact much?" was the reply.

I wasn't overreacting. At least I don't think I was. An incomplete sentence would be like singing, "shave and a haircut, two ..." and stopping there. It hangs on our psyche like a loose toenail or a squeaky wheel. It must be right or we'll obsess over it. Or, more accurately, I will obsess over it.

I wrote to this person one more time, adding a grammatical itch that cannot be scratched, "Understand your position," I wrote. "Also, I hear tomorrow will be partly sun..." Never did hear from her again.

CROWD ESTIMATES ON THE FLY

A local Nashville television reporter covering a visit to the city by President Trump wrote the following Tweet, "A member of the 118th Wing tells me there are at least 200 hundred people gathered [at the airport] to bid [the President] farewell." How many people? It's either "200" (and it's ok to use the Arabic numeral in this case), or "two-hundred." Unless the reporter meant 200 *times* one hundred, meaning there were 20,000 people at the airport. Surely that would be the largest bidding adieu crowd ever ... period.

OLYMPIC AERONAUTICS

The aerial light shows at the opening ceremony of the 23rd Winter Olympics in PyeongChang, South Korea were a technological wonder. Over 1,200 lightweight drones—each capable of displaying several different color lights—flew in perfect synchronization and forming, at times, a dove, a snowboarder, even the interlocking Olympic rings.

The drones worked using technology developed by Intel Corp. It involved sophisticated software to create the detailed three-dimensional flying images. Video games aside, who needs virtual reality when you have Intel-powered light shows?

The show itself was not live. Unfriendly weather conditions forced the TV networks to broadcast a recorded flying performance. It was still an impressive show of beauty and technology.

ABC News aired a very good story about the flying light show. While explaining the world-record-setting technology,

Senior National Correspondent Matt Gutman said those 1,200 drones can be flown by "fewer than two pilots."[2]

Wait. How does one have "fewer than two" pilots? Isn't that the same as one?

Merriam-Webster defines "few" as a small number.[3] It can be used as an adjective, as in "may I ask a few questions?" and as a pronoun, as in "the discriminating few were in attendance."

From a grammatical standpoint, Gutman's usage of "few" was spot on. But how does one employ fewer than two pilots? What's the other pilot doing when they are not flying? To find out, I went straight to the horse's mouth (a phrase, by the way, originating in horse racing circles whereby tips on which nag could win logically comes from trainers or those closest to the horse's mouth itself.)

Intel's own promotional video about the drones talks about the logistical challenges of setup and flight. It also says the drones are flown by a single pilot (which *is* less than two). Gutman's terminology can be forgiven. Intel's video shows scores of people setting up the drones and testing the software.

And the term "fewer than two pilots" may have originated in some press release. I am reminded of an adage from the public relations business: if you hold a press conference and eight reporters show up, your response to the client's question of "how many reporters were there" is always "about 12."

AUTHOR'S NOTE: My critique of Matt Gutman was not appreciated by one reader who works in TV news and who took the time to write and say I just did not understand how hectic things can be when a television news broadcast is coming together. I appreciate the sentiment, but I doubt putting together a TV news broadcast is markedly harder than putting together a daily newspaper. Different? Yes. Harder? Nope.

THE NTH DEGREE

A colleague received a confirmation letter for her toddler's day-care orientation. The nicely organized material noted that the orientation would take place promptly on "September 21th." That's the number 21 followed by "th" in superscript.

I'm not even sure I can pronounce that number.

Putting superscript text after a numeral is called an ordinal number. Saying one, two, three, etc. is using a cardinal number, which refers to quantity. An ordinal number—first, second, third, etc.—refers to the distribution or order of the number.

Our language is absorbent. "All right" eventually became "OK." "United States of America" eventually became "USA," and on and on. And because our language is absorbent, and changes to the language happen organically, somewhere along the line an ordinal indicator—a letter or group of letters—latched on to numerals to represent ordinal order, as in 1st, 2nd, 3rd, 4th, 5th and so on.

The construction "21th" in my colleague's letter, had it been spelled out, would have been incorrectly represented as "twenty-oneth." The correct construction is "twenty-first" or "21st."

Construction of Cardinal and Ordinal numbers is simple, but here's a cheat sheet nevertheless:

NUMBER	CARDINAL	ORDINAL
1	One	First
2	Two	Second
3	Three	Third
4	Four	Fourth
5	Five	Fifth
6	Six	Sixth
7	Seven	Seventh
8	Eight	Eighth
9	Nine	Ninth
10	Ten	Tenth
20	Twenty	Twentieth
100	One hundred	Hundredth

And so on.

Let's write—words and numbers—carefully out there, people.

ℰ

swear it out

PROFANITY CAN BE A REAL CLUSTERF&%K

Swearing is not uniquely American. It was an Italian lexicographer who first entered the word "fuck" in the dictionary in the 15th century (and not, I assume, because he stubbed his toe).[1] But we Americans do profanity rather well.

One hundred years ago, H.L. Mencken said, "The average American, I believe, has a larger profane vocabulary than the average Englishman, and swears rather more, but he attempts an amelioration of many of his oaths by softening them to forms with no apparent meaning (Darn becomes Durn, for example), and while *damn* is apparently of English origin, it is heard ten thousand times in America to once in England."[2]

And it ain't just an observation from 100 years ago. To wit:

Mr. Spock: [Admiral] your use of language has altered since our arrival. It is currently laced with, shall we say, more colorful metaphors, "double dumb-ass on you" and so forth.

Kirk: Oh, you mean the profanity?

Mr. Spock: Yes.

Kirk: Well, that's simply the way they talk here. Nobody pays any attention to you unless you swear every other word.

—STAR TREK IV: THE VOYAGE HOME[3]

Yep, we love our cuss words.

Fun sidebar #1: Hollywood legend says that while filming the 1991 movie *My Girl,* cast member Jamie Lee Curtis insisted there be a "swear jar" on the movie set to minimize the amount of what she called "trucker talk." Curtis' real reason was to prevent her own overuse of profanity. "My mouth has its own fan club," she allegedly once said. At the end of production, Curtis gave $200 to her two ten-year-old costars, Macaulay Culkin and Anna Chlumsky, then—as the story goes—she told both to F-off.[4]

Fun sidebar #2: *Ball Four* author Jim Bouton said the manager of the Seattle Pilots (now known as the Milwaukee Brewers), Joe Schultz, preferred saying "shitfuck" in place of an expression like "what the heck" (or something nastier). Bouton said that members of the Pilots would therefore affectionately refer to Schultz as "Old Shitfuck."[5]

Fun sidebar #3: Every one of the "seven dirty words" that

comedian George Carlin used in his monologue about words you cannot say on television are indeed in the dictionary? Yep, shit, piss, fuck, cunt, cocksucker, motherfucker, and tits can all be found in *Merriam-Webster*. No mention of whether they can be said on television.

We find profanity both shocking at times and funny. But when profanity moves from the spoken to the written or broadcast word, something happens. We clutch. We gasp. We say you cannot do that. We're in shock when a microphone picks up Joe Biden telling Barack Obama that passage of the Affordable Care Act is "a big fucking deal,"[6] or when U.S. Senator from Michigan Carl Levin describes a piece of pending legislation as "a shitty deal."[7] The *Columbia Journalism Review* once opined that being shocked at foul language in online news stories is questionably hypocritical, since some (many?) of us may be reading that news story after browsing fetish porn. (No judgment here, folks.)

FROM A BARNYARD EPITHET TO A CLUSTERFUCK

New York Times reporter J. Anthony Lukas found himself in a linguistic pickle over 50 years ago while covering the trail of protesters accused of disrupting the 1968 Democratic National Convention in Chicago. The defendants continuously shouted "bullshit" in court, causing more than a little consternation amongst the prosecutors, judge, and everyone else present.

"When the time came to file my story, I realized the trial that day was spent debating the use of a word *The Times* wouldn't print," Lukas recalled during a speech before college journalism students in 1977. *The New York Times* may consider itself the newspaper of record, but not all the news was fit to print in the late 1960s.

Lukas solved his dilemma by changing the word "bullshit" to "a barnyard epithet." That phrase became the title of his 1970 book about the trial of the Chicago 8.

A half century later *The Daily Tar Heel*, the independent newspaper of the University of North Carolina, had no hesitation over printing an obscenity when it described UNC's efforts to reopen the school amid the COVID-19 pandemic this way: "UNC has a clusterfuck on its hands."[8]

The message was abundantly clear. Trying to open the campus amid the worst viral pandemic in over 100 years was not working. The same day that headline appeared, UNC decided to switch to online classes only.

There is no question that the intended message was delivered. But was the delivery vehicle—use of a vulgar term in print—the best grammatical avenue to take?

To be clear, I am not criticizing *The Daily Tar Heel*. Anyone who knows me knows I am no altar boy when it comes to how I talk. Also, clusterfuck is indeed a word. Its first usage, according to *Merriam-Webster*, was in 1969 ... probably describing *The New York Times'* internal debates over printing the word "bullshit."[9]

Most readers applauded *The Daily Tar Heel's* choice of words. "I preach you shouldn't swear in news copy," one reader posted on Facebook. "However, if you choose to do it, it must serve a narrative purpose, punctuating and lending urgency to your point. I'd say these kids got it absolutely right."

"Cursing, if you choose to employ it, should be oral," says Neill Borowski, owner and editor of the online news site 70and73.com and a former college newspaper editor. "When you utter the f-word, it comes and goes in an instant. Any shock tends to be short-lived. In a news headline, it's in front of you and doesn't go away. It's like uttering the curse over and over."

Another Facebook member posted about the headline and included a photo of abandoned newspaper vending boxes in her neighborhood. She wrote, "It's sad that this era of local news is behind us, though given the amazing reporting by *The Daily Tar Heel*, I'm hopeful that journalism isn't dead."

> AUTHOR'S NOTE: In the spirit of good reporting, I did try to get a comment from *The Daily Tar Heel*, reaching out to the editors via Twitter, email, LinkedIn, Facebook, and this age-old communications tool called the telephone. No one responded.

Almost two years before *The Daily Tar Heel* used one word to describe an utterly disoriented and mismanaged situation (that's *Merriam-Webster's* definition of clusterfuck, by the way), Americans were slack jawed over the moment when the President of the United States allegedly referred to third world countries as "shitholes." During a meeting at the White House in January 2018, President Donald J. Trump reportedly called nations in South Africa as well as Haiti and El Salvador "shitholes" during a discussion about immigration.[10] I say "reportedly" because those who initially say they heard Trump cuss have recanted their statements or found themselves a victim of political liability memory—that memory that kicks in whenever the truth may get you in trouble. (That's my definition, at least.)

In the days and weeks after that first report in *The Washington Post*, there were nearly 2,500 stories in the news about President Trump's use of the word "shithole." (I know because Michael McCluskey from the University of Tennessee at Chattanooga counted them. Thanks, Mike.) The stories, McCluskey says, basically followed one of three themes:

1. OMG, did you hear what he said? (That's my paraphrase, not his exact term.)
2. Is this the United States' policy toward immigrants from these countries?
3. Is saying "shithole" really a Presidential thing to do?

The reaction throughout the country was profound. People clamored and wrote to their Congressmen. (Me, too. I wrote a letter of complaint to U.S. Senator Lamar Alexander, and he wrote back, calmly saying that, yes, I'm right. People shouldn't swear. Thanks, Lamar.)

After all that hoo-ha over the "shithole" remark, I'm betting you probably don't remember that 18 months later President Trump tweeted the word, "BULLSHIT" (yep, all caps) when describing the ongoing efforts to impeach him. This is a wild guess, but I'm thinking THAT wasn't Presidential, either.

In the spirit of fairness, Trump is not the only President with a potty mouth. Harry S. Truman referred to General Douglas MacArthur as a "dumb son of a bitch."[11] John F. Kennedy, upon hearing that his wife had spent $5,000 refurbishing part of Air Force Once, remarked that "this must be a fuck up."[12] And Lyndon Johnson, explaining why he didn't want to fire FBI Director J. Edgar Hoover, said, "Well, it's probably better to have him inside the tent pissing out, than outside the tent pissing in."[13]

There is a subtle difference I think everyone is missing. It may be news when a public figure or celebrity curses. (Ever hear

Taylor Swift cuss in public? She does it so seldom that *BuzzFeed*, in a post by writer Ryan Sockett, wrote a "Every Time Taylor Swift Has Cursed" story.[14]) It is one thing when there is a story over someone cursing, but what about using profanity to actually tell a story?

Profanity can elicit strong reactions. But as Neill Borowski said in AFWAW, when spoken, it dissipates and goes away. In print, it sticks around, and when uttered live on television, it has a much stronger impact. Other than *The Daily Tar Heel*, we don't typically find news organizations using profanity to tell a story. If the thermostat outside hits minus 10 degrees in the winter, the local meteorologist doesn't come on TV and say, "It's fucking cold outside, people!"

It seems there is an unwritten line of demarcation between reporting a profanity if it is a direct quote and using the profanity to tell a story. Trump allegedly calls third world countries "shitholes," and it seems to be OK to report that because you're using it in a direct quote. But *The Daily Tar Heel* wasn't quoting anyone. They used the word "clusterfuck" to make a point.

In 2019, when the world marked the 50th anniversary of the moon landing, *The Onion* published a faux front page that read, "Holy Shit. Man Walks on the Fucking Moon!"[15] Like *The Daily Tar Heel*, that use of profanity did tell the story, but unlike *The Daily Tar Heel*, it was meant for comedy.

For the most part, news organizations deftly dance around using a direct profanity. In early 2019, the *New York Post* reported updates on a story about Amazon founder Jeff Bezos, who was allegedly blackmailed by the *National Enquirer*. That newspaper was reported to have pictures of Bezos in the nude and having sex with his mistress. Bezos successfully called the

Enquirer's bluff and the *Post's* headline about this story read "Amazon Chief: *National Enquirer* boss tried to blackmail me with nude pics ... Bezos Exposes Pecker."[16]

Ah, so the *Post did* use profanity, didn't they? Not quite, although they came close. The chief executive officer of American Media, publisher of the *National Enquirer*, is a fellow named David J. Pecker. (Yes, I know, his name is "Dave Pecker." I'll take names that get my high school ass kicked for $10,000, Alex.) The *Post* was using his last name in its headline as a clever double entendre.

The 2018 retirement of U.S. Supreme Court Justice Anthony Kennedy marked a moment when President Donald Trump could appoint a conservative justice to the court, tipping the balance on the court to very conservative. Knowing this was on the horizon, *The Daily News* in New York City flashed the following headline, complete with a caricature of Trump wearing a judge's curly wig: "We are F*#%D."[17] Again, the *Daily News* did not use the profanity, but the point certainly got across.

Not all news organization are pristine about profanity. In 2014, the news website *BuzzFeed* released its own guidelines for profanity in a new style guide. Unsurprisingly, the guide takes a unique approach to cursing.

BuzzFeed's guide contains proper style for "fuckup" as a noun, "fuckup" as a verb, and "fucked-up" (hyphenated, notice?) as an adjective. It has spellings for "shitlist," "shitstorm," "shitshow," and "shithole." And "shit talk" has space when used as a noun and a hyphen when used as a verb.[18]

I'm not sure if this is a cultural shift, where we're getting comfortable enough with profanity that we're mainstreaming it. The Society of Professional Journalists' code still has the following four elements: seek the truth and report it, minimize harm, act independently, and be accountable (to the audience and each other).[19]

We're still making sure that we are not doing harm and being accountable. Almost, but methinks not quite. We should not think society is sinking into a profanity pit. Here's why: I started a social media promotion at Vanderbilt University where students would take over the school's Instagram account for a day. It was a good way to show what life is like on campus from a student's point of view.

In the days leading up to the takeover, Vanderbilt would make sure to announce in advance that it was a student who would be posting on a specific day, and the student's name and photo would be posted well ahead of takeover day. There were some written guidelines for posting, since Vanderbilt's college of education often had young children on campus, and their photos could not be used without parental permission. One thing that was not included in the written directions, though, was restrictions on language.

I knew we could not stop a student from posting profane language. After all, freedom to post whatever they wanted was the whole point of the promotion. But I had confidence that as intelligent college students they could find other ways to express themselves ... even if that expression was meant to be a forceful opinion. Guess what? This promotion has been going on since 2016 and, to the best of my knowledge (I retired a year after starting this), not one student has used profanity. That's some clever shit, huh?

I'll leave this discussion about profanity with an insightful observation from one of the readers of my newsletter. After the issue of AFWAW about *The Daily Tar Heel* was posted, I received a thoughtful response from writer Joe Ovelman, who said, "I wrote about a publication quoting someone's use of the word 'fag' but printing it as 'F--.' We see it all the time, too, 'the F-word,' 'the N-word.' Use words carefully, for sure, but when we've made the decision to use the word, print the word. Words aren't scary, people using words are."

Let's write carefully out there, people.

9

don't label "dis" language

DISSING INTO DIS SUBJECT

After writing a professional endorsement letter for a colleague, I copied and pasted the letter into an email to her and wrote in the subject line, "How's dis?"

I hit the send key before I could stop myself. Not only did I use slang (honest, I try not to when writing), but I think I used a slang term not commonly accepted.

Dictionary.com and *Merriam-Webster* define "dis" as a form of the words disrespect, disparate, or belittle.[1] Its origins are traced to the early to mid-1980s, where it is extracted from those two aforementioned words. But I used it as an alternative for the word "this." In the case of my errant email, I meant to say, "How's this?" which obviously isn't one of the definitions used. Or is it?

I have seen this term online, where usage such as, "dis my sister" or "dis my new ride," crop up. And as I have noted before, language evolves. Karl Sornig, writing in 1981 about the evolution of slang terminology, said:

> Whereas the linguist may not even doubt the rules he himself has projected onto an existing and working linguistic system, the language users may very well transcend the norms and that have hitherto been valid for his own strategical beheviour. Using language is like using a tool or playing a game: any competent participant may apply norms as he thinks fit and thus slightly modify if not the norms themselves, at least the relevance and predominance of certain of them within the system.[2]

Translation: if a word can be twisted to some other meaning, then twist away.

Rusty Barrett, a professor of linguistics at the University of Kentucky, explains in an email that the use of "dis" in more elegant terms. He says the two forms of "dis" are typical examples of truncation, just like the word "mic" is a truncated form of the word "microphone."

"The 'dis' used in place of 'this' is part of a common dialectal pattern where the voice 'th' sound in standard English corresponds to [the sound of the letter d]," he explains. "Since the 'd' pronunciation is common in working-class varieties, it is often used to convey stereotypes associated with working-class communities, like toughness and urban coolness."

Dr. Barrett notes that fans of the New Orleans Saints and the Cincinnati Bengals in the National Football League use different truncated spellings of "that" and "they." Saints fans are fond of saying, "Who dat?" and Bengals fans like saying, "Who dey?" "The forms reflect stylistic choices that draw on the cultural associations between innovative forms and particular social groups," Barrett says.

Dis all means I was not off-kilter when I may have accidentally dissed my colleague. As long as my endorsement did not say, "who dey sayin' she's no good?" I think I'll be OK.

WHO SAID IT FIRST?

One day the talking heads on CNN were discussing the U.S. Senate confirmation hearings for United States Supreme Court justice nominee Brett Kavanaugh, and the conversation centered around sexual harassment. One talking head mentioned the confirmation hearings for Associate Justice Clarence Thomas in 1991 and said, "I think that was when the term 'sexual harassment' was first coined."

Was it? At the risk of being accused of mansplaining (a term absorbed into the language in 2010 whereby us dudes take the mic and explain everything), I decided to check the way back machine—the internet to most people—and see when that term first entered the lexicon.

It appears to have come from Cornell University in the mid-1970s when journalist Lin Farley was discussing workplace experiences with female students.[3] She found that every student in this gathering was either fired or had to quit a job because they refused the sexual advancement of a superior. From there the phrase "sexual harassment of women at work" emerged.

That may be the genesis of the term. Sadly, the practice goes back even farther.

FORMERLY KNOWN AS

After enduring years of relentless accusations that the team's name is racially insensitive, the National Football League franchise in Washington, D.C. on July 13, 2020, announced it was dropping the team name "Redskins." No new name has emerged; instead, the plan would be that, for one season, the team will simply be known as "Washington."

But that did not deter one local television news anchor who delivered the news about the Washington team hiring its first Black head of football operations by leading into the story saying, "The team formerly known as the Washington Redskins today ..." It is interesting that the news anchor used the team's old name to identify it. I mean, a sports story wouldn't identify the Tennessee Titans of the NFL by calling them "the team formerly known as the Tennessee Oilers," would they?

(For the football-impaired among us, Nashville's NFL franchise originated in Houston, Texas in 1960 under the name Houston Oilers. The team moved to Tennessee in 1997 and for two seasons they were known as the Tennessee Oilers until changing the name to Tennessee Titans in 1999.)

Before anyone emails me saying, "Well, *what* should the local news guy say?" consider what David Muir on ABC News did that very same day when he reported the same story by saying, "Washington, D.C.'s NFL franchise today ..." Options, folks. There are always options.

A WORD ABOUT LABELS

If someone tells me they grew up in Chicago, I will for fun ask them if they are a Cubs or a White Sox fan (that's baseball, folks). If they say Cubs, then chances are they grew up in one of the suburban towns surrounding Chicago. Conversely, die-hard White Sox fans often grew up within Chicago's city limits. Obviously, there are exceptions, but that rule of thumb largely holds true.

Labeling anyone like that also can be fraught with mistakes. For example, I grew up only 50 miles from Yankee Stadium. So, one would assume I am a New York Yankees fan. I'm not. I have been a Boston Red Sox fan since 1967. My affection for the Olde Towne Team has a lot to do with my Dad being a Yankees fan. I went in the opposite direction. But I'm digressing again, aren't I?

Anyway, my point is that labels can be misleading. They can also be annoying.

In 1988, a six-year-old in Philadelphia named Ralph Brooks was the victim of a drive-by shooting.[4] Sadly, he was left partially paralyzed and has had difficulty walking ever since. The shooter was caught and put on trial, and Brooks was required to testify. Every story in the news thereafter (or at least it sure seemed this way) referred to him as "Little Ralph Brooks."

Fast forward about 30 years, and a five-year-old boy in Dickson County, Tennessee, Joseph Clyde Daniels, went missing. His father, Joseph Sr., was arrested and charged with the murder of his son.[5] While the case is still pending as I write, the young boy is constantly referred to as "Baby Joe Daniels" in news stories.

In both cases, one would think the youngster's names were "Little Ralph" and "Baby Joe." Those are labels that can be hard to shake.

In the spirit of misleading labels, a study by Kathleen Hall Jamieson of the University of Pennsylvania and Dolores Albarracín from the University of Illinois suggests that, in the early days of the COVID-19 pandemic, those whose political affiliations tend to lean more toward Republican thought the virus as a hoax. Those leaning toward Democratic thinking felt it was real. Their survey of over 1,000 individuals found that those leaning Democratic sourced their news from NBC and/or *The New York Times,* while those leaning Republican sourced their news from Fox News.[6]

No political statement there. Just sharing the results of the study.

FALLING FLAT ON PRONOUNS

CNN's Chris Cuomo once tried a joke that fell flatter than a pancake. In the early days of the 2020 Presidential campaign at a CNN LGBTQ town hall, then U.S. Senator Kamala Harris said her pronouns were "she, her, and hers." This is a nod to the fact that non-binary individuals will use the plural pronouns "they, theirs, and them" in singular usage when referring to themselves.

Cuomo tried making light of Harris' statement and said "she, her, and hers? Mine, too."[7]

First, please know that there is nothing new about using the plural pronoun "they" for singular usage. Emily Dickinson was doing it over 100 years ago. Second, identifying one's personal pronouns is not some trendy idea. I participated in seminars on this topic whilst working at Vanderbilt University, where I learned this is a way to show respect toward others.

To his credit, Cuomo apologized for his gaffe. And, yes, "his" is indeed one of Cuomo's preferred pronouns.

Channeling my inner Ask Abby, it is perfectly acceptable when meeting someone to not only say what your preferred pronouns are, but to ask the individual what theirs are as well.

NEW LANGUAGE FOR THE PANDEMIC

The Earth was turned upside down several times over throughout the early 2020s when a seemingly unstoppable virus appeared and spread throughout the world faster than anyone could imagine. The scariest aspects of the most frightening movies and novels about viral infections could not hold a candle to what the world witnessed in places like Wuhan, China; Milan, Italy; and New York City. At one press conference, the President of the United States appeared visibly shaken when he told everyone that the coming month of April 2020 would be, "Tough. Very tough."[8]

It was nightmarishly hard. I lost several friends to COVID-19. I watched the news slack-jawed when New York sent the National Guard into New Rochelle in a fruitless effort to seal off that community and stop the spread of the virus. My wife and I took turns going to the grocery store, an undertaking that felt more like we were making a supply run in a zombie apocalypse movie than it did a visit to the market. We were asked to stay home. Keep our kids home from school. We didn't see our grandson. We did all that and, while looking out our windows, we thought the world looked largely the same. Until we attempted to go out and received side eye for wearing a mask. Or for not wearing a mask.

And through it all, we developed or refined new terminology, phrases, and nicknames. We learned that the term "coronavirus" is lowercase because it is a generic term. We learned it is called the "novel coronavirus" because its unique properties are still being understood. And we capitalize COVID-19 because it is an abbreviation for "CoronaVirusDisease-2019."

We also coined a slew of new terms. Useful? Yes. Humorous? Sometimes, which is as good a way as any to get through a crisis. Here is just a smattering of the pandemic lexicon.

Flatten the curve, which is a term used to describe efforts to slow down the rate of COVID-19 infections. Visualize a bell curve with the peak of the curve being the point where hospitals can (or cannot) accept any more patients without risking lives. Flattening the curve keeps that apex below the danger zone.

Pandemic, which as an adjective refers to something prevalent over an entire country or the world. As a noun, pandemic is an outbreak of a pandemic disease. Of course, pandemic differs from ...

Epidemic, which is an outbreak of disease that attacks many people at about the same time and may spread through one or several countries.

Underlying health conditions, I'm not sure how often we heard this term before the pandemic, but I did a bit of digging to understand its usage. "Underlying" is the present participle of "underlie," meaning something beneath something else. It also can refer to a steady, truss, or a way to bolster or carry. In the case of the current health crisis, the first definitions seem to work best.

Social distancing, which *Merriam-Webster* says was first used in 2003, roughly coinciding with the SARS outbreak.[9] It is the practice of maintaining a greater than usual physical distance from other people or of avoiding direct contact with people or objects in public places during the outbreak of a contagious disease to minimize exposure and reduce the transmission of infection.

Asymptomatic, which *Merriam-Webster* defines as presenting no symptoms of a disease.[10] This is one of those words of efficiency. Rather than saying, "He has no symptoms," you save a couple of words by saying, "He's asymptomatic." Then again, what are we saving those extra words for?

Elective surgery, which refers to a surgical procedure one chooses to do and does not involve a medical emergency. Elective comes from the Latin "eligere," meaning to choose. Types of elective surgeries can vary from cosmetic to orthopedic and more. Fifteen years ago, for example, I had surgery to repair a torn rotator cuff. As much pain as I was in leading up to the surgery, that was still an elective procedure.

Diagnostic test is the one with the swab that goes up your nose—far enough up that you think the back of your brain is being scratched and is used to determine if you have COVID-19.

Antibody test is the one with the blood sample to determine whether you already had COVID-19.

Other new terminology creeping into our lexicon include:

- Zoom: Honest, what I would have given to be an investor in this company back in December 2019.
- N95 mask: I had several of these in my garage because I'd wear one while cutting the grass. Like investing in Zoom, I would have loved to have been an investor.
- Curbside pickup
- Curbside drop off
- Safe at home

- Virtual doctor visits
- Super spreader
- Fauci
- Birx
- Six feet
- Outdoor only
- Paperless purchases
- No touch services
- Test queue
- Swabbing
- Herd immunity
- "Handle your own balls" and "wash your balls" (Sign at a golf course. No, I am not making this up.)

HUMOR WILL GET US THROUGH IT

Maureen Boyle, a longtime friend, college classmate, and author of the wonderful book, *Shallow Graves: The Hunt for the New Bedford Highway Serial Killer*, reports she's discovered the word "foofaraw" and promptly posts to her social media followers that she plans to use it every day. "You have been warned," she writes.

"Foofaraw" means a great deal of fuss given to a minor matter. Seems appropriate for a fellow wordsmith. Speaking of fuss given to seemingly minor matters, more than a few terms about the pandemic randomly used by the proletariat continue to come across my desk. Let's delve, shall we?

Ticking up or down? A reporter for a local television station, talking about the rate of positive COVID-19 tests said, "the uptick is going down." Reporting in a pandemic does nasty stuff to good grammar practices.

Covidiots. I first heard this whilst watching a daytime television talk show. (Hey, there are only 52 episodes of *Downton Abbey* available to stream, so gimme a break on my TV watching.) The Urban Dictionary defines a covidiot as someone who ignores the warnings of public safety, or who hoards goods ... yes, like toilet paper.[11] P.S.—I have never watched *Downton Abbey*. Sue me.

Mind your gerunds. A political commentator—it doesn't matter if the person leans red or blue—recently tweeted, "It's time to start the reopen of America." This individual used an infinitive ("to" plus a base verb "reopen") when a gerund was required (verb plus "ing"). Using "reopen" would work had the pundit said, "It's time to reopen America." But they didn't. So there.

House arrest? The same pundit said most of America was "under house arrest" due to social distancing. *Merriam-Webster* defines house arrest as being held in one's house against their will with a guard outside making sure no one leaves or has an ankle monitor slapped on the leg just above the Louboutin's.[12] There's no guard outside my house. Just my neighbor's cat, "Bingo," who thinks he owns the street and takes umbrage with anyone who walks by. Like most people, I come and go as I please. But given the prevalence of COVID-19, I am pleased not to come and go.

English equivalent? There is a German term, *kummerspeck*, which translates to excess weight gained from emotional over-eating. There isn't an English equivalent, but I kind of like "grief-bacon," signifying all the trips we're making to the refrigerator, as an English version.

Latin comes in handy sometimes. The pastor at my church—I catch his sermons via YouTube nowadays—used the term "liminal space" in a recent sermon. Liminal comes from the Latin word "limen" and means a threshold or the space between what was and what's next. We certainly are in a liminal space as we wait out the pandemic.

Pandemic word of the moment: From *The Skimm*, *maskne*: a skin condition brought on by wearing a mask. Let me stop here and offer an important Public Service Announcement: I am no doctor, but I am sure maskne mostly happens to healthcare workers or anyone who wears a mask for eight to 10 hours a day. It *will not happen* when you wear a mask just to go to the store.

Not a term, but it's still sound advice: Japan takes preventing the spread of COVID-19 seriously, even to the point of making sure no one shouts, thereby increasing the distance covered by droplet infection (yes, that is a thing). A sign at a theme park in Japan reads, "please scream inside your heart."[13] Show of hands, who from March 2020 onward wasn't screaming on the inside?

Abundance of caution: Anybody else notice this went away sometime in June 2020?

Coronacoaster: a noun referring to the ups and downs of a pandemic. One day you are loving life in the bubble, working out, baking bread, going for long walks. The next day you are depressed, drinking wine by the box, and missing people you don't even like.

Gender rules: COVID-19 is a feminine term, so says the Academie Francaise of France, and should be used with the article "la" rather than "le."[14] And that is as much as I shall touch *that* hot potato.

Headline: "U.S. asks dead taxpayers to return relief checks." Did the government use a Ouija board to ask?

On or in line: Are we waiting "on" line for a COVID-19 text, or "in" line? Waiting on usually means one is waiting for step one to take place before step two can happen. Waiting on also means one is being attended to (like having a Q-tip shoved up your nose, which I suspect is something we don't mind waiting for). The judging panel rules in favor of waiting on line for said test.

Categorizing the funny stuff: *The New Yorker* magazine carried a list of new language of the pandemic in its July 2020 edition.[15] Here are a few samples:

- Body mullet—what we wear for Zoom calls; work clothes on top, gym shorts (off camera, we hope) below.
- Maskhole—someone wearing a mask in a way making it ineffective: below the nose or below the chin.
- Parenting—figuring out why the PlayStation isn't working with your WiFi.
- COVID-30—Two months ago this was the COVID-15, but all that sourdough bread we're baking is having an effect.

I HATE EMOJIS

Psychologists in Israel surveyed over 500 people from 28 countries to determine their reactions to the use of emojis in business correspondence. The results? There's no reaction to the use of an emoji in a happy email, but there is a negative perception of the writer if an emoji is used in a serious email.[16] This is one of many reasons why I don't heart emojis.

But people do use them, which led to a discussion in one issue of *A Few Words About Words.*

I'm old school on a lot of things pertaining to the written word. Emojis, those pictures on our smart phones depicting laughter, sadness, and other emotions, are not considered language, according to the *English Oxford Living Dictionary,* because they cannot, on their own, convey messages.

Still, emojis may be here for the long term. *Harper's Magazine's* "Index" notes that 7.2 out of every 10 people in Great Britain prefer emojis over words. Apparently, people are becoming more and more comfortable communicating with them.

Also, they enable fast-paced communications. The January 4, 2018, sports section of *The New York Times* carried a Major League Baseball story about how the Miami Marlins consummated a trade with the Seattle Mariners for outfielder Dee Gordon. The final approval was a short text, via an airline's onboard Wi-Fi service, using a "thumbs up" emoji.[17]

Trendy emojis have staying power, and some terms that enter the lexicon can become a permanent part of the language. By the way, the most popular term to enter the lexicon the year I was born (no, I will not say what year) was "nit picker." Is anyone who knows me surprised by that? I didn't think so.

They are being taken seriously. Researchers in Australia are investigating the use of emojis to evaluate how young children understand and experience well-being by helping make children active participants in the research process. The researchers looked at how emojis can help identify a young child's (age three to five years) understandings and experiences. Their research showed that emojis can become the voice of a young child.[18]

But they also can be vague. An emoji smiley face can, simultaneously, convey a despising, mocking, or obnoxious attitude. The story in the *Times* mentioned a different situation where an athlete's agent responded to a contract offer with a "thumbs up" emoji. Did that mean they received the offer or that they agreed to the terms therein?

Writers should step gingerly into the use of emojis for business communication. *Fast Company* published a useful "do and don't" guide for emojis in written communication. It offers common sense tips, including do use them to convey humor, but don't use them when corresponding with someone you may not know or a strait-laced co-worker, like your boss.[19]

Attorney M. Shute, Jr. of Nashville acknowledges that symbols have their place in legal communication. Using an "X" for a signature can be acceptable for legal correspondence, provided there are witnesses attesting that the "X" is indeed that individual's mark. Technology like DocuSign uses a symbol of one's signature to make communication legally valid within an email.

"There is some level of emotion involved," Shute said, noting that he worked with a client in the music business who was building out details for a tour. "He responded with heart emojis to the suggestion of some dates and venues, but he still needed a contract with the tour dates in it somewhere. You need to understand that emojis won't show up or hold up in a court of law."

UNCOMFORTABLE CONVERSATIONS

Do we say Black or African American? I found a clear answer thanks to Emmanuel Acho, former National Football League player and current sports commentator for ESPN, in his video series, "Uncomfortable Conversations with a Black Man."

The short answer is to say Black. It is most accurate and least offensive. "Not all Black people in America are African," he explains in one video. "They can be Cuban, Jamaican, but also some Blacks choose to not identify with African because they may feel slavery stripped away that identity."[20]

Khadijah White, Ph.D., a professor at Rutgers University, notes that "Black" is a statement of identity that emerged from a particular historical context and moved away from outdated terms such as "Negro."

And it is "Black," with an uppercase 'B.' In early 2020, the Associated Press changed its position on this, explaining that saying "black" (lowercase) is a color, not a person. This change comes on the heels of major news organizations changing their writing style to use uppercase Black when describing an individual. (There also is an argument that "White" should be initial cap when talking about a person. There will be more on that to come, I am sure.)

Inadvertent or underlying prejudices often show up in journalism. Dr. White, a former television news reporter herself, recalls the time a reporter at a television station where she worked was interviewing a survivor of Hurricane Katrina in New Orleans. The survivor, an older Black woman, addressed the young white reporter as "Mr.," yet the reporter referred to the woman by her first name throughout the story, a departure from how the show typically treated interviews.

"It amazed me. They treated her as though she didn't have a last name," Dr. White says. "And I was the only person who seemed to notice." She also points to inconsistent treatment of people in news stories based on race. She recalled a news story about two low-income families: a white couple who had several children and a black woman who was a single mother. "The reporters asked the single mother why she was pregnant, but they never asked the family that same question about their reproductive choices," Dr. White said.

"EXCEPT FOR" AND WHITE ALLERGIES

In Acho's video he discusses "white allergies," which are proof that words can hurt. "The greatest white allergy I see is back-handed compliments," Acho says. "[In] high school they'd say to me, 'Acho, you don't even talk like you are Black,' or 'You're like an Oreo. Black on the outside and white on the inside,' or 'You don't even dress Black.' I realized that [they] were assuming that Black people don't sound educated ... you are assuming something about Black people, and I contradict that assumption."

Acho's video series can be found on his website and YouTube. It is worth subscribing to.

#SAYTHEWORD ALREADY

I am, as I am sure we all are, familiar with the subject of political correctness, or P.C. I'm not an expert, but I am familiar.

For example, someone isn't short, so goes the joke, they are "vertically challenged." I am bald, but the P.C. police prefer I say that I use more toothpaste than shampoo. (OK, I made that one up, but I *am* bald, or hair follicle challenged.)

Some commonly used P.C. terms include visually impaired ("blind" is only used when the individual cannot see anything), hard of hearing (similarly, "deaf" is only used when the individual cannot hear anything), intellectually disabled, and "handi-capable" for someone who is physically impaired.

Do these terms go too far? A group of researchers thinks so. An article in *Rehabilitation Psychology,* a journal of the American Psychological Association, argues that "disability" isn't a dirty word and is perfectly fine to use in place of clunky terminology like "handi-capable," "differently-abled," and even "physically challenged." Not using the word "disability" can have unintended and adverse consequences.

"Decisions about language have important sociocultural meanings in the disability community, and erasure of the term 'disability' can evoke fear and frustration among those who claim a disabled identity and align with disability culture," the authors say.[21]

"Having a disability is not something to be ashamed of," says Anjali Forber-Pratt, Ph.D., a professor at Vanderbilt University's Peabody College and one of the six authors of the article. Forber-Pratt and her co-authors all identify as disabled. Forber-Pratt is a former Paralympian and studies identity development at Vanderbilt. The authors are promoting a #SaytheWord social media movement to embrace disability identity.

"The field of psychology has a rich tradition of appreciation of cultural diversity and individual difference," Forber-Pratt says. "Yet, disability has largely been left out of these efforts. The disability movement is moving toward the status of a diverse cultural group with a social justice agenda parallel to those of other marginalized communities."

The article promotes use of the social media hashtag #SaytheWord to encourage everyone to be comfortable using the term disability, and the hashtag has started a conversation. "I prefer 'disability' to 'unique challenges' or 'special needs' or 'extraordinary.' Disability isn't special. It's normal," one person wrote on Twitter. "DISABILITY is not a dirty word!! 'Access Inclusion Seeker' is just offensive," said another person.

By the way, Major League Baseball has ceased referring to a list of players injured and unable to play as the "Disabled List" and instead calls it the "Injured List." I'm all for baseball standing up to #SaytheWord.

Let's write carefully out there, people.

10

festivus, a collection of grammatical pet peeves

IN MID-DECEMBER ONE YEAR, I found myself hunting for a topic to write about for the January issue. That was when my sister posted something on Facebook asking people to partake in "Festivus," the airing of grievances. It was a fun social media post based on an episode of the TV sitcom *Seinfeld*, where people would gather around a table at the Costanza's house at year's end, break bread, then air their grievances about anything and everything. The late Jerry Stiller, playing the character Frank Costanza, would stand at the table and shout, "I've got a lot of problems with you people, and you're gonna hear about it!"[1]

Each episode of the show "Seinfeld" was only 22 minutes long, but it was easy to fill that time with people airing whatever was getting under their skin.

Well, my readers and I have more than our share of problems

with our language. I was stockpiling my own list of grammar grievances, and figured I'd create my own holiday tradition—a Festivus issue.

Readers happily sent me their own grievances. They're not shy about offering advice on future subjects, such as:

- Can you make people stop saying "preventative"? Say "preventive" and it'll do just fine.
- Since when do we wait ON something?
- "Anyways" is a real thorn in my side!

Anyways, since I seemed to be waiting on a good idea, I figure a preventative step would be to cobble these grievances together for all to share a kvetch about. Here are but a few from past Festivus issues of AFWAW. It worked.

Double-check the dictionary

To say, "It is comprised of…" is wrong. "It comprises" is correct. *Comprise* means "made up of." You already used the word *of* by saying "comprise;" saying "comprised of" is, therefore, redundant.

Fight the rise of double negatives

Double negatives never go away. On a recent local TV news broadcast, I heard, "He was suspended for improper misbehavior." Really? Was he helping a little old lady across the street rather than throwing Molotov Cocktails at some storefront?

Note: My advice about avoiding double negative was challenged. Readers wasted no time informing me that Mick Jagger is living large 50-plus years after singing he "can't get no satisfaction," *and over 400 years ago Shakespeare made Viola say, "And that no woman has; nor ever none shall be mistress of it." Clearly, I doth protest too much if I darest argue with the Bard of Avon. And Mick **is** an alumnus of the London School of Economics.*

Proper list construction, part one

Use parallel construction when writing out lists. I love lists. But I hate it when they are improperly constructed. Begin each list point with an action verb (Run, Edit, Create) or a noun (Dogs, Cats, Rainbows), but *be consistent when you do this*.

Proper list construction, part two

While I am on the subject, who tossed punctuation out the window when stuff is in a list? Use a period at the end of each list point. Conversely, construct the list as a long sentence, using the correct punctuation (comma, semicolon) at the end of each point. Then begin the final point with the word "And," since you are essentially breaking up an "A, B, C, and D" sentence into bullet points.

Stand your ground, part one

Be prepared to politely and respectfully disagree when the client trashes your efforts to explain their jargon-entrenched technical product or service in plain, straightforward language. "My audience will understand/know what this means," they usually say. With all due respect, if the audience *did* know or understand, then you wouldn't need a writer. Or a brochure. Or a website.

Stand your ground, part two

Remember, though, in the end it isn't *your* product or service you are writing about. Explain your position, but make it clear you will respect the client's opinions and direction.

Don't be obsessed with jargon and acronyms

I worked for IBM, DuPont, and Vanderbilt University: three businesses (Egad! I just referred to a college as a "business." Somebody grab the stoning bucket.) which may hold a three-way tie for the championship of jargon, although Peabody College within Vanderbilt University (By definition, a "university" is a collection of individual colleges banded together under one flag. Or, nowadays, one marketing slogan. Now you know.) has an inside edge. Peabody maintained an ever-growing database of acronyms. It was around 80 or so at the time when I found it on the college's website. Peabody College even maintained a spreadsheet one could download to see what each acronym stood for.

Forgive me for asking, but wouldn't it be easier just to follow the Associated Press rule of spelling out the acronym on first use, then using the mysterious acronym afterwards? In the case of Peabody College, the answer clearly is no.

I think we are obsessed with making words into acronyms because it's a way to quickly coin new terms. You probably know that "laser" once was an acronym for "light amplification by stimulated emission of radiation," and that "scuba" was "self-contained underwater breathing apparatus," and that taser was "Terry A. Swift's electronic rifle." (No, it's "Thomas," not Terry, so you *did not* know that last one. Stop nodding.)

Acronyms and related jargon often place a stranglehold on our writing, making fuzzy that which should be clear. While at IBM, a co-worker was trying to write a press release about a new mainframe computer IBM was about to unleash on the market. I remember seeing my poor co-worker standing toe-to-toe with one of the product managers, arguing about the language in the press release. "You don't understand," the product manager shouted, his face red and sweat beading up on his forehead, "the press release HAS TO BE confusing to read!!" Honest that happened.

Later, when I was freelancing, I worked with a team at IBM who prepared software applications for automobile manufacturers. Every time I'd write something using what I thought was clear, straightforward English, my work would come back, marked up and jam packed with jargon. "My customers talk this way," the sales executive said. "We have to use this language." Should I point out that this team missed their sales goals and is long gone from IBM?

Proper names that were once capitalized become lowercase words

Unless it is at the beginning of a sentence, "internet" takes a lowercase "i." *The New York Times* and the Associated Press say so.[2,3] It is not trademarked, and it has become common language. Must be something about new technology that makes us want to capitalize stuff. "Phonograph" was once initial cap, so was "Telephone." A good perspective on this can be found in Carolyn Marvin's wonderful book, *When Old Technologies Were New.* You can better appreciate how society incorporates technology into everyday life after reading it.

Stop beginning a sentence with the word "so"

So, I know we love using this word. So, think about this. So, if we just removed the word "so" from the beginning of each sentence, would the sentence sound any different? So, would those sentences sound better? So, should I stop using the word so, so much? So, let it be written. So, let it be done.

Note: In the newsletter, I hyperlinked that last sentence to a short YouTube video of a scene from the 1956 movie, "The Ten Commandments," where Yul Brynner, portraying Pharaoh Ramses, utters the line, "So let it be written; so let it be done." If it works for pharaoh ...

And by the way, if you remember the movie, Moses didn't stay banished for long, and the Israelites were eventually freed. It just shows that, like language, no rule is absolute.

Remember that language is always evolving

William Safire wrote volumes about how language is continually changing. Remember earlier in this list I said the word "Phonograph" was once initial cap? Language changed. Be flexible, but always keep your copy of *The Elements of Style* handy. Those rules haven't changed since 1935.

Readers are not shy about reaching out to me. After the first Festivus issue was published, I received a one-line email from a reader, a former doctoral student I knew at the University of Pennsylvania who I always admired for her professionalism:

"I LOVE THIS NEWSLETTER!"

I knew then that I was on to something good. Should I repeat this issue? Maybe make it an annual thing? Again, that's flattering *and* scary. But finding fodder to gripe about seems too easy.

IF IT WORKED ONCE ...

In college, I took a class on the business of magazines, taught by a talented adjunct whose name, sadly, has escaped me. But I vividly remember one thing she said about developing content for magazines. "If an idea works once, it'll work two times, three times, four times, five times." She would slam the palm of her hand on the desk as she counted, just to drive the point home.

Know what? She was spot on. I decided to repeat my post-Christmas celebration of Festivus. Here is more from the Festivus celebration.

THEY ARE GRADUATES, NOT A CHEMICAL

A dean at an institution of higher education where I worked (I worked for Harcum Junior College, Vanderbilt University, and the University of Pennsylvania. Let the guessing games begin*.) frequently referred to a graduate as an "alum." This highly educated person isn't alone in making that mistake. The word "alum" is short for potassium aluminum oxide, a colorless astringent compound that is a hydrated double sulfate of aluminum and potassium, used in solution medicinally and in dyeing and tanning ... and that is more than you probably ever want to know about alum.

(*And the games did commence. In a period of less than a week after this item appeared in the newsletter, I received dozens of emails from co-workers at Vanderbilt, Penn, and Harcum College, all playing an almost desperate game of whodunnit. Don't worry, Michael, Mike, Camilla, Joan, Ed, John, and the other academic deans I know. Your secret shame is safe with me.)

However, an "alumnus" is a male graduate. An "alumna" is a female graduate. "Alumni" is the plural for male and female graduates, while "alumnae" is the plural for female graduates.

I just explain the rules. I don't make them.

By land or by sea

Whenever there is a tragedy—plane crash, shooting, passing of a notable person, the flag is lowered in honor of those who have passed. Remember, though, that lowering the flag on a flagpole that is in the ground is lowering it to "half-staff," whereas lowering it on a boat is "half-mast."

How many times do I have to say it? Language continuously evolves

This topic is not exactly one for the language evolved group. There are those who would argue that the pronoun "they" is plural. Yet the use of "they" as singular, especially for non-binary individuals, is largely accepted today. Language evolves and absorbs over time. *Merriam-Webster* notes that use of the word "they" as a singular pronoun has been going on since *at least* the year 1300.[4] So "they" as a singular pronoun evolved. Some of us have not, I guess.

Stop relying on spellcheck

This is a good resolution for everyone. A flyer for a New Holland, Pennsylvania charity's open house said, "Donations Excepted." Spelled correctly, all right, but a bit confusing to the reader.

Conversely, stop and **look** when that red line shows up under text. An on-screen graphic accompanying a TV news story about a big game between the Tennessee Titans and the Indianapolis Colts said post-game coverage would include "Players Reax." The word "reax" appears in the Urban Dictionary as an alternative to "reaction."[5] Go slow with absorbing new words.

Especially for those of us (like me) who are slang-challenged.

Speaking of typos, believe it or not, there are a few recipients of my newsletter who decide they don't like it and opt out of the distribution list. Yes, I'm shocked too. One person opted out by writing, "Too many emails. I grt over 100 a day." Apparently, none of those emails are about proofreading.

Proofreading doesn't have to be solely correcting misspelled words. It can also involve catching errors in syntax. The community pool and playground in my subdivision has the following warning sign posted: "Area closes at dusk. Violators will be trespassed." I'm not sure what that punishment is like, but it doesn't sound pleasant.

Run-on sentence of the year does not go to CNN

Some readers asked if there can be a "Run-on Sentence Award" and that Maeve Reston of CNN be given the inaugural honor for something written in late 2020.

Ms. Reston, writing about the January 5, 2021, U.S. Senate runoff election in Georgia, penned this lengthy one-sentence tome:

> With the eyes of the political universe, focused on turning out voters in Georgia -- where the two runoff elections will determine which party controls the U.S. Senate -- the President's relentless attacks on the state's voting apparatus, its tabulating process, and its Republican secretary of state are prompting handwringing among GOP strategists and state leaders who fear those attacks are eroding confidence in elections at a time when they need to turn out as many of their voters as possible to reelect Republican Sens. Kelly Loeffler and David Perdue on January 5 and hold onto their firewall against a Democrat-controlled House and White House.[6]

Funny thing: Reston did not write a run-on sentence. The strict definition of a run-on sentence is when two sentences are smashed together without a coordinating conjunction or proper punctuation. Reston's sentence, while long and potentially leaving readers exhausted, would not draw a "tsk-tsk" from Miss Thistlebottom, since it is properly punctuated and holds together from a grammatical standpoint.

That missive COULD have been broken into separate sentences. Like this:

> The eyes of the political universe are focused on a turn out the vote effort in Georgia. That's where a January 5 runoff election will determine whether Republicans or Democrats control the U.S. Senate. President Trump's relentless attacks on the Georgia secretary of state and the overall voting apparatus might erode confidence in elections precisely when incumbents Kelly Loeffler and David Perdue need that confidence. If voters believe Mr. Trump's rhetoric, then they may stay home on January 5, thereby hurting Loeffler and Perdue's chances of victory. Their loss would hand the Senate to Democrats.

Interchangeably? I think not

"Can we get reporters to stop using 'uncharted' and 'unchartered' interchangeably?" one reader asked.

Both words are adjectives, but the similarity ends there. The word "uncharted" means an area not mapped or previously surveyed and is normally but not exclusively a nautical term. Conversely, "unchartered" means having no charter or constitution. Once again, in nautical terms "unchartered" would refer to the part of that famous three-hour tour where the Minnow wound up on a heretofore "uncharted" island.

Stop taking the gloves off

One quirk of our language that should go away is the phrase "taking off the gloves" in political reportage.

To be polite, it is overused. "Clinton escalates her smear campaign; Sanders takes the gloves off," "Donald Trump is taking off the gloves," "The Clintons are taking off the gloves," and "Hillary Clinton and Donald Trump are taking off the gloves," are a handful of headlines from the 2016 presidential campaign.

To be impolite, it's like there is one key on every political reporter's PC that spews out that line with a single keystroke. A Nexis Uni search by my colleague, Melissa Mallon, at Vanderbilt University uncovered scores of times the phrase was used during the 2016 presidential campaign.

The term is a colloquialism, used to indicate that someone has decided to stop being the nice guy in a political fight. Its first usage appears to have been in *The Nottingham Guardian* from April 20, 1866, when it reported, "[T]he gentleman who came to show the excited state of the town was obliged to admit that on the 26th of June he used to the excited people of the town the expression about taking off the gloves and breaking the buttons from the foils."

I have chided writers in the past for a lack of creativity in social media posts ("I'm proud to be …", "I'm excited to be …", "So honored to …," please make it stop.). Let me offer the same admonition to those covering a presidential campaign; there are other terms you can use.

- "They are no longer being nice, as if they ever were."
- "If voters thought it was nasty before, they ain't seen nothing yet."
- "Nasty comments abound on the campaign trail."
- "Covfefe" (OK, not that one. But it WAS only used once!)

SOME MORE STUFF THAT CAME OUT DURING THE HOLIDAYS. GET OUT YOUR EDITING PENS.

The holiday season! That time between the day after Halloween and New Year's Day. We shop for gifts. We bake. We pull out the ugly holiday sweaters. (I guess. I have never owned one.) We celebrate by breaking bread with family and friends. We exchange gifts. We say goodbye to the old year and welcome in a new one.

But more than anything else, we're writing. A lot.

For starters, we're writing messages on holiday cards. The U.S. Post Office handles about *two billion* holiday cards every year. Every one carries a message written by both the card manufacturer ("Wishing you a Merry Christ-Mouse," says the one with a mouse wearing a Santa cap. Corny, I know, but you get the idea here.) and the sender. We rarely just sign our names; we add short notes to personalize each card.

Show of hands: Who gets bored writing the same thing on every card and instead gets the urge to write, "Yes, yes, yes, the family is well. Check with Cousin Debbie and she can fill you in." So, we mix it up a bit. A message about the kids on this card, a message about a new job on that card.

While I am on this topic, who has ever wondered if someone sends conflicting messages about the family to different people? You know, telling the aunt you never see that Gramps has a twenty-something girlfriend, but telling the cousin you see every weekend that Gramps and Gram are doing just fine. Anybody? Am I the only one?

Even preprinted cards have a message somebody wrote in advance. Those printed messages are marketing messages of one sort or another.

Marketing messages can be found in abundance during the holidays, which remain the biggest shopping time of the year. After shopping on Fifth Avenue in New York City on the day after Thanksgiving, I thought the day was called "Black Friday" because of the size and fanaticism of the crowds at stores who are all frantically seeking the best available bargains. Years later, I learned it refers to retailers finishing the year with their financial books "in the black" thanks to that one day.

But that time of year also prompts a slew of holiday marketing slogans. Most are pretty good. ("A hug is the perfect Christmas Gift. One size fits all. It can be returned.") Other, perhaps, are forgettable, ("Without you, all I am is helpless.") but hundreds are concocted every year.

What better time of year to showcase our writing prowess or ineptitude. Greeting cards? The annual family holiday letter? Marketing slogans? There is no end to the places where grammar can be trod upon by the masses.

One editor said I should start this chapter with observations on family holiday letters, those wrap-the-year-up-in-two-single-spaced-pages missives that everyone seems to dread. My initial response was, "Let's not." I know I am not alone in my dislike for these things. My wife, who is a kind-hearted soul and loves to hear updates from friends, hates ... I mean *h-a-t-e-s* holiday letters. She usually refuses to read them or delays doing so for as long as possible.

I suspect holiday letters are something everyone thinks about writing the moment they get one from a friend. ("Johnny, the cousin you've never heard of, finished basic training while Mandy, the other cousin you never knew existed, was cut from the cheer squad for drinking, but that's just how life folds together, isn't it?") Now that I re-read that last sentence, I think *that* would be a fun holiday letter.

I'll offer the following advice on holiday letters because I doubt I can convince anyone to not write them. Shorter. And if you refuse: subheadings. Lots and lots of subheadings so your loved ones can pick and choose what parts of the letter they want to read. And I am sure eventually someone will read the whole thing. Honest, they will (nudge-nudge, wink-wink).

My favorite movie quote list

I'm a sucker for holiday movies. Doesn't matter how often *Miracle on 34th Street* comes on television, I'm watching it.

I'm also interested in how each word of any movie script can serve a purpose. The late Gene Siskel, film critic for *The Chicago Tribune*, was a stickler for movie scripts that were tightly wound, never wasting a word.

It's with an eye for the not-wasted-word that I take a critical look at some holiday movie favorites.

Not a ninnymuggins was stirring

It's the holidays! Time to visit the Redbox DVD dispenser and grab a few seasonal favorites—*Elf, The Santa Clause, Die Hard* ...

Some of these cinematic masterpieces contain phraseology or terms that have an interesting history. Here are a few examples.

"I'm a cotton-headed ninnymuggins!"

—WILL FERRELL'S CHARACTER, BUDDY THE
ELF, IN THE 2003 MOVIE *ELF*.[7]

Believe it or not, "cotton-headed ninnymuggins" has a lexico-graphic history and isn't just a term the scriptwriters dreamed up. "Cotton-headed" is an old insult meaning "airhead." The term "ninny" refers to a fool, while a "muggins" is a foolish or gullible person. When you are 915 off your Etch-a-sketch quota, the term fits.

"We field-dressed a cat."

—TIM ALLEN'S CHARACTER, SCOTT CALVIN, IN
THE 1994 MOVIE *THE SANTA CLAUSE*.[8]

This is one seriously gross line. And it comes from a family-friendly movie, no less. Field-dressing means removing a critter's innards right after it has been shot dead. Yuck! But happy holidays, folks. Bring the kiddos.

Not all of the script will gross you out. Allen's character uses several names that have been used to identify Santa Claus over the years (sans the "e," which is included in the movie title because it refers to a clause in a contract), including:

- Kris Kringle, traceable to the German term "Kristkindl," meaning "Christ Child."
- Sinterklaas, which is the basis of a mythical holiday figure in the Netherlands and Flanders. There, Sinterklaas walks across roofs, finds a shoe that children leave for him, and places presents in the shoe.

- Père Noël, who is the gift-bringer in France and other French-speaking territories.
- Babbo Natale, which is Italy's version of Santa. By the way, La Befana, an old woman who delivers gifts on the Epiphany (which is on January 6; stop Googling it), is more popular there than Santa.
- Pelznickel, the crotchety fur-clad gift-bringer in the palatinate region of southwestern Germany.[9]

"Yippee-ki-yay."

—BRUCE WILLIS AS JOHN MCCLANE IN THE
1988 ACTION FILM *DIE HARD*.[10]

OK, put down the pitchforks and other blunt objects. *Die Hard* is humorously considered a Christmas movie, even though it was released in July. The use of "yippee-ki-yay" was a sarcastic reference to the main character's alleged love of Roy Rogers movies.

The yip part of "yippie" originated in the 15th century and refers to the sound of a small bird.[11] The use of "yippee" was first used in a Sinclair Lewis novel, *Main Street*, where he wrote, "She galloped down a block and as she jumped from a curb across a welter of slush, she gave a student 'Yippee.'" The full term first appeared in an old Bing Crosby song, "I'm An Old Cowhand."

Interestingly, Roy Rogers never uttered that term in any of his movies. Honest, go back to Google and look. For the record, Trigger, his horse, never said it, either.

WHAT DO YOU CALL SANTA'S ELVES? SUBORDINATE CLAUSES!

Rudolph, the red-nosed caribou: Yep, the correct name for Santa's reindeer is caribou. The word "reindeer" has roots in the 15th century from an old Norse word that grew out of the phrase, "hreinn reindeer," which was used to identify a male caribou.[12] You can thank the advertising team at Montgomery Ward department store in Chicago for creating the story of Rudolph. The tale of the red-nosed caribou was used by the retailer in its 1939 holiday advertising campaign and was later converted into the well-known song by … anybody?

Hint: it wasn't Gene Autry, which so many people seem to think. Rudolph was the creation of advertising guru Robert May, who wrote the story, and singer/songwriter Johnny Marks, who put the whole thing to music and probably lost a ton of royalties after Bing Crosby recorded the song. But there I go digressing again.

Baubles hanging from the tree: A bauble is defined as a trinket. Its origin goes all the way back to the 14th century when it was described as a piece of jewelry, as in "he affixed the bauble, with a kiss, upon her finger." It was Sir Walter Scott who referred to the scepter brandished by a court jester as a bauble. Interestingly, an ornament for a Christmas tree is the *fourth* and final definition offered up by *Merriam-Webster*.[13]

We kiss under the mistletoe, *why?*: Mistletoe is considered a hemiparasitic plant that grows on pine, oak, birch, and apple trees. It's called a hemiparasatic plant because it carries out photosynthesis independently but obtains water and minerals from the tree it is attached to. So basically, mistletoe is a leech. The business of giving your bestie an "um-wah!" on the cheek when beneath the mistletoe comes from a Celtic tradition of placing a small amount of it above the doorway to homes during the winter.

It was considered a sign of life therein despite the dreary weather because mistletoe remains green year-round. The thought was that hanging it over the doorway ensured harmony within the premises. Giving the resident a kiss probably helped promulgate said harmony.[14]

Gold, Frankincense, and Myrrh. Or, in current terminology, money and first aid: Think about the gifts from the three wise men. Gold, I get; giving money as a gift is both safe and a no-brainer, even if the recipient uses it to buy mayonnaise. WebMD defines frankincense as a hardened gum-like material that is made from cuts in the trunk of a Boswellia carteri tree.[15] WebMD also describes myrrh as a resin from bark.[16] It's used to treat indigestion, colds, even colic. Having had a newborn with colic, I *know* that's a great gift, one that's worth more than gold. Money and medicine; those three men were wise indeed.

I am no different than anyone else who doles out advice during the holidays. Go easy on yourself. Remember that writing is not a natural act, and the end of the year surprisingly calls for a lot of writing. With all the other pressures that come upon us, we should not plotz over doing something we may not be the very best at doing. Besides, if everyone did write carefully out there during the holidays, then I would have nothing to write about myself.

STOP NEGLECTING YOUR KNOWLEDGE

While this never appeared in a Festivus issue, it is one of my ongoing pet peeves—someone writes something just *assuming* they have their facts straight. A Vanderbilt professor puts those wrong-minded writers in their place. She coined the phrase "knowledge neglect" to explain why smart people can make mistakes over what seems like common knowledge.[17]

Lisa Fazio, an assistant professor of psychology at Vanderbilt, shares a simple three-question quiz to make her point:

1.	How many animals did Moses take on the Ark?
2.	Which museum houses Michangelo's portrait of the Mona Lisa?
3.	What phrase followed, "To be or not to be" in Macbeth's soliloquy?

Fazio says you probably shared answers like, "two of each," "the Louvre," and "that is the question." Gotcha! Noah built and piloted the Ark, Leonardo da Vinci painted the Mona Lisa, and it was Hamlet who posed the question. Fazio calls these easy to make mistakes "knowledge neglect," whereby we have this knowledge in our heads, but we fail to use it. She postulates that this goes a long way toward explaining why so many people seem to be fooled by misleading news stories on social media.

Fazio also says repetition solidifies beliefs. In other words, if we keep saying Moses built the Ark, then we'll eventually believe it. Fazio's advice is, "Rely on your brain, not your gut."

TEST YOUR KNOWLEDGE NEGLECT

Below are a series of statements. Decide if they are true or not.

1.   The Great Wall of China is NOT visible from space.

2.   John Glenn was the first American in space.

3.   Jackie Robinson was the first Black man to manage a Major League Baseball team.

4.   George Washington signed the Declaration of Independence.

5.   Alaska is the 51st state.

6.   There is an even number of red and white stripes on the American flag.

7.   The abbreviations "i.e." and "e.g." mean the same thing.

8.   Irregardless is not a word.

9.   You can use the term "each other" when talking about three or more persons.

10.   If "coziest" is the superlative of "cozy," then "bestes" is the superlative of "best."

ANSWERS

1.   True. Other than city lights, nothing man-made is visible from orbit.

2.   False. Alan Shepard was the first American in space. Glenn was the *third* American to fly in space (Gus Grissom was the second), but he was the first to orbit the Earth.

3.   False. Robinson was the first Black man to play in the Major Leagues, but Frank Robinson, in 1975, became the first Black man to manage a Major League team.

4.   False. Washington was busy commanding the American army as it battled the British.

5.   False. There is no 51st state. Alaska is the 49th state, joining the U.S., just eight months before Hawaii became the 50th state.

6.   False. There are 13 stripes, signifying the original 13 colonies. Seven stripes are red, six are white.

7.   False. "i.e." means "that is" or "in other words," whereas "e.g." means "for example."

8.   False. It's been a word for nearly 250 years.

9.   False. "Each other" pertains to two individuals. Add one or more persons, and you would instead use the term "one another."

10.   C'mon, you're killing me Smalls. "Best" is the superlative of "GOOD."

//

the final word

We're all writers, aren't we?

EVERY WRITER'S DILEMMA

When you finally get the grammar right—and sometimes even when you do not have it right—it's time to start writing. Professional basketball hall of famer Julius Irving is credited with saying, "Being a professional is doing the things you love to do, on the days you don't feel like doing them." Writing is no different. It's a muscle you must keep toned. And writing every day is the way to do that.

Despite the long hours writers put into their craft, their skills can be misunderstood, misused, and unappreciated.

Here is my "for instance." A request came to me via telephone from a tenured member of the faculty while I was working as director of communications at the University of Pennsylvania's Annenberg School for Communication. Yes, I was "director of communications" for a school of communications. Let the puns fly. I have heard them all.

Anyway, the professor asked, "Joe, can you help me edit something?"

Amazing, I thought. *A world-renowned communications scholar wants my opinion on something he wrote! This is the greatest day of my life!*

OK, OK. It wasn't the greatest day. That honor goes to getting married closely followed by my daughter being born. Still, it felt cool to think that a scholar wanted my help writing something. Until, that is, I tried to help.

I suggested he email his draft to me, and I would look at it right away.

"No, no. Just listen to what I wrote," he said as he started reading in a rapid-fire, staccato voice. He rattled off eight to ten paragraphs of text before coming up for air and said, "Does that make sense?"

He read so fast his words ran together. I honestly had no idea what he had just read to me. I again asked if it were possible for him to email his draft, explaining that I could do a better job if I could see his copy. Alternatively, I offered to walk upstairs to his office (he was literally one floor above me) and look at it.

"No, no, no. You're the writer here. Just listen and let me know if it makes sense." This gentle tug of war continued for several minutes: him reading text—faster each time—me asking him to re-read something because I was having trouble hearing the words and envisioning them on a page. Finally, after sensing that he was becoming restless with my multiple requests to re-read something to me, I surrendered to the fact that, working this way, there was no way I could add value to his prose. I sighed and said, simply, "Sure. It's good. Really."

He was understandably disappointed with my tepid response. But not so disappointed that he demurred from doing the same thing with me again and again over the eight years I was his colleague. In fact, he wasn't the only professor to do that. Multiple times I would be asked for assistance, only to have my help rebuffed or ignored before I started. More on that in a moment.

That brief memory encapsulates the best and worst thing about being known as a writer. Your skills may be respected— which I suspect is why the professor called me to ask for my opinion—but you often cannot perform at your best, as in this case where I felt I was being asked to edit blindly.

Mind you, I did not begrudge the professor's request. He respected my ability and genuinely wanted my help. I have worked with many college professors, and most are a true delight to know. I have collaborated with several to write newspaper op-eds and even helped edit some of their academic papers. Some even admit their subject matter limitation. "I have a tremendous amount of knowledge about a very narrow subject," says Jessica Taylor Piotrowski, Ph.D., Director of the Graduate School of Communications at the University of Amsterdam. "I like to remind my doctoral students of that every day."

There have been more than a few occasions when writers encounter people who don't appreciate what writers do. Some work in academia, others work in the private sector.

THE ANTSY PROFESSOR WHO REALLY HATED MY WORK

About 25 years before that experience at Penn, I was in Cambridge, Massachusetts meeting with an astrophysicist at the Massachusetts Institute of Technology. I was writing an article for IBM about how MIT faculty were using IBM computers to help identify signs of life in the cosmos. This very intense professor—she conducted herself as though a lynch mob was closing in on her at any moment—was explaining how using powerful telescopes and deep space radio signals, her team could determine the chemical makeup of planets and deep space objects based in part on the light color the telescopes detect. Some chemical makeups emit different lights, giving scientists a clue as to what they are seeing. It also is an important step in determining where signs of life may exist in space.

"So, you are telling me that based on what color light you see, you can determine what makes up the object in space, be it a planet or star or asteroid, correct?" I asked to confirm.

"Well, it's more complex than that," she said. I could see she was already looking down her nose at me. I was nevertheless determined to write a good article that she would approve easily. My job in those days was to find interesting and newsworthy uses of IBM products. Using an IBM computer to search for aliens certainly fit the bill.

After talking to her for about an hour and taking copious notes, I went back to my office and wrote a story explaining that the chemical makeup of objects in space is essentially color coded. I sent my draft of the story to the professor to get her corrections and, hopefully, approval.

Based on her reaction to what I wrote, you would have thought I was suggesting we eat babies on live television. She refused to even send the article back to me, sending it instead through the third party who had set up the interview. This third party—an IBM salesperson who made the initial intro-ductions—said the professor was quite upset over what I had written, that I did not understand what her work is about, and, therefore, she did not want to continue talking to me.

By the way, today there is agreement that the electromagnetic spectrum in space has different degrees of light and color. Hydrogen (reddish), Sodium (yellowish) and Magnesium (green to blueish). So, it *is* color coded.[1] Take that, MIT professor-who-hates-me.

READERS WILL HYPOCRITICALLY CONTRADICT YOU

One of my first big freelance writing assignments was for a former employer, IBM. I was hired to write press releases about a series of new products the company was about to bring to market. New product announcements by computer companies were considered serious news stories in the early 1990s, and IBM wanted to make a big splash. One of the products was a robotic system designed to retrieve magnetic storage tapes. Again, in the early 1990s, companies still stored a lot of their data not on the cloud but on reel-to-reel magnetic tape.

My client asked me to write the press release in a way that *The New York Times* might report the story, omitting the usual corporate jargon. It seemed an easy enough project. The draft of my press release started out something like this: "IBM today announced its first-ever robotic magnetic tape retrieval system ..."

The line of business executives responsible for the new products at IBM hated what I wrote. "The news is that we are leading the industry AGAIN!" one shouted.

Ultimately, the final draft of the press release started out saying IBM was continuing its leadership position in the production of magnetic tape storage systems with a new solution for data retrieval. That isn't the exact opening, but "leadership," "innovation," and other jargon had worked its way into the final draft. (My client, feeling bad about the negative reaction my first draft received, sheepishly apologized for even asking me to write a *New York Times* version of the press release in the first place.)

Twenty-four hours after the announcement, *The New York Times* ran a story about the news from Big Blue. This isn't the word-for-word transcript of the news story, but it basically started out this way: "IBM today announced its first robotic data storage ..."

Yeah, basically what I wrote. My tongue still hurts from having bitten down on it so hard.

"WHAT YOU WROTE IS FINE, BUT IT SUCKS."

The last freelance assignment I worked on before taking a job at a P.R. agency was for a company that built shipping and packaging systems for rolls of steel plating. They wanted a brochure on their shipping solution, as they called it.

I had learned from my IBM freelance work to add jargon, so I wrote a brochure with some company jargon sprinkled in.

The client said I left out several important points, then began verbally citing a list of the topics I had omitted.

Funny thing, each topic he said was missing *was* in what I wrote. I kept pointing out that my "omissions" were inclusions. It turns out he simply did not read what I had given him.

Finally, after the back-and-forth between us ended, the client sighed and said, "Well, I asked my secretary to write something, and I think I'm just gonna use what she did."

That was nearly 30 years ago, and I still can't bring myself to comment any further on it.

THEY WILL INSIST YOU GOT IT WRONG

Even when you get everything right in a story, someone may criticize your efforts. In 1978, I worked as a newspaper reporter in Bridgeport, Connecticut. I and several other staffers at *The Bridgeport Telegram* were covering a very contentious strike by the city's public-school teachers. Relations between the teachers' union and the city had become so bad that the city was throwing teachers in jail for not doing their jobs.[2]

The animosity between the teachers and the city continued while the union leaders were in the slammer. During one negotiation session taking place in the prison, a fistfight broke out between the president of the teachers' union and the lead attorney representing the city.

I wrote about the fight the day after it happened. I was confident in my reporting because I had *three* eyewitness sources; two agreed to go on the record—a teacher (who, coincidentally, was the ex-wife of the teachers' union president) and a representative of the state teachers association—and one confirmed the fight off the record (the attorney for the city ...the one who was throwing the haymakers ... and who begged me not to write the story lest his bosses discover his unwarranted fisticuffs).

I decided to write the story because it demonstrated how far apart both sides were, and it gave an indication of how long schools were going to remain closed. Guess what? Despite having a Woodward and Bernstein caliber set of sources, several persons—including members of the newspaper staff where I worked—said the story was wrong. I stuck by my guns, and the story was never retracted.

CONVEYING COMPLEX INFORMATION IN SIMPLE TERMS

Mea culpa: I am as guilty of judging someone by their writing as that MIT professor. More than once, after reading something another party wrote, I have come away thinking that what I was reading truly was written by a room full of chimpanzees chained to typewriters. But I don't react the way this MIT professor did. I wait until I have a chance to capture it in a book manuscript.

In my long and unspectacular career, I have often interviewed someone for a story who says something to the effect of, "I don't see how you can write clearly about this. I *can't*, so how can you?" (Actually, there was only one person who said that to me. He hated what I wrote, too.)

Mort Walker, the comic strip genius behind "Hi and Lois" and "Beetle Bailey," used to run story arcs in "Beetle Bailey" where the soldiers at Camp Swampy would engage in nonsense activity while the base commander, General Halftrack, was around. Not wanting to seem like an idiot and feeling he should know what was going on, General Halftrack would look upon Beetle and his comrades and say, "You're doing it exactly right."[3] I think about that whenever someone I am interviewing says they cannot clearly explain what they do for someone trying to write about it. I am going to out on a limb here and suggest that maybe if what someone is doing cannot be explained, it may be because they don't understand what they're doing, either.

That is the nature, for better or worse, of writing. Sometimes you can't satisfy the customer because what so many writers hear—"I know what I like when I see it"—is really true.

BUT IT'S LIKE CHOCOLATE MILK WHEN THINGS GO RIGHT

But I don't despair, and neither should any aspiring or veteran writer out there. For every MIT professor, software designer, and auto break manufacturer there are positive experiences.

There is Arco Chemical, which for many years in a row asked me to write an aspirational speech for their chairman to use when he thanked volunteers with the company's speakers bureau. They were ordinary employees who took the time to meet with schools, community groups, and others. I never met face-to-face with Alan Hirsig, CEO of Arco Chemical, when I prepared for and wrote those speeches, but to know he asked for my work year after year was one great rush.

My favorite good news about writing a story comes from Siemens Healthineers, a PET/CT scanner manufacturer I had the pleasure of interviewing a few years ago. They wanted a humanist story on what went into designing and building the most accurate PET/CT system ever made. Sure, there was a lot about the size and number of crystals used in the lenses, a lot about the various mixtures of injectors (the radioactive material shot into the patient to get a picture of their innards), but what the client really wanted was something about the dedication involved in building the system ... from the entire team.

I spent one very long day interviewing a dozen or more people. I asked questions like why do you do what you do? What ignites your personal fire within? Why does what you do make a difference? The feedback I received from the team was insightful, enlightening, and heartwarming.

- I learned from a product team leader about a PET/CT technician who had cancer and had diagnosed it himself, discovering his condition was terminal. This fellow's dedication to his profession nearly brought the team leader to tears. "I followed him for the rest of his clinical course until he passed away," he said.

"I have always thought that if I can live up to his example of how to deal with something so potentially devastating as the diagnosis of cancer and still maintain enough presence of mind to be rational and fight 100 percent of the way, then I can do something that really matters. I will remember this guy for the rest of my life. What he did. What he taught me."

- I learned how one principal developer of the PET/CT scanner was himself a cancer survivor and how a scanning system that gives quick and accurate answers can deliver profound peace of mind to patients.

- I learned how the four-year-old son of one team member, a fellow who held a Ph.D. in chemistry, would walk around telling people he was going to be a doctor like his daddy so he could help people, too. "That's all the motivation I ever need," this fellow said.

- The story about how the PET/CT team eagerly provided warm blankets for a patient who had volunteered to test the scanner.

And all of this made its way into the story. And the client loved it. It's still posted on the company's website. When you have that kind of humanistic insight, the technical stuff in the story takes care of itself.

I have encountered every end of the writing spectrum and many, many points in-between. What they all tell me is what I learned years ago: Writing is not natural. It's hard. But dedication and enthusiasm and interest in the rules of grammar can leave us with something quite beautiful.

It all comes down to writing carefully out there, people.

a note from the author

IN THESE PAGES I talked about how writing is not a natural process, how there are rules, and how those rules are either mistakenly broken or how they can evolve over time. What I haven't said is that writing can be fun. William Zinsser is half right. Writing is work, but it's also fun.

<u>Exhibit A:</u> In the summer of 2020, ABC television affiliate WKRN in Nashville covered a clay pigeon shoot charity event sponsored and run by Mike Fisher. Most Nashvillians know of Fisher. He is a retired National Hockey League player, having played nearly 20 seasons for the Ottawa Senators and later for the Nashville Predators. He's also the husband of country music star Carrie Underwood. One could argue that Underwood easily noses out Fisher on the fame scale. While I have paid

to see Mike Fisher and the Nashville Predators at Nashville's Bridgestone Arena, I have only once paid to see Underwood in concert. Ironically, it also was at Bridgestone. Underwood is good, but she probably has a lousy slap shot.

During an on-camera interview Fisher discussed the genesis and benefits of this charity event. Typically, the lower third for the type of interview Fisher did would simply include his name and perhaps the words "charity founder."

In this case, however, the lower third included these memorable words: "Mike Fisher. Still married to a famous person."

Well, they aren't wrong. The person who wrote that lower third had some fun while informing the viewers.

Exhibit B: I once quoted Homer Simpson in the lead of a press release, written for a University of Pennsylvania psychology professor. The professor's research suggested younger people's brain development can lead to bad decision making. The quote was Simpson's line, "To alcohol! The cause of, and solution to, all of life's problems."[2] I never thought the press release, which discussed research by an Ivy League school professor, would be approved. Guess what? It was.

Having fun while writing does not mean ignoring the rules of grammar and even logic. I attended a sales conference where the emergency evacuation directions included with the conference overview paperwork told people to PLACE EMERGENCY PROCEDURES HERE. Admit your mistakes and move on. Which brings me to:

Exhibit C: Among the many things that went into developing the popular Jungle Cruise ride at Walt Disney World was a script for the "captain" of the cruise boat to follow. One part of the script identifies an animatronic "chief" of the local tribe as "CHIEF NAME." The idea was to let whoever was piloting the boat make up names as they saw fit. But in a short time, the local chief's name simply became "Chief NAH-MEE."

Our first job as a writer is to convey facts in clear and concise terms. It does not mean we have to be dull.

So, keep writing. Have fun. And let's write carefully out there.

acknowledgments

IT TAKES A LONG TIME and an array of family, friends, and colleagues to bring a book to life. My own team comprises many: my parents, who always insisted that I get better grades in school than I was getting; Father Diaz at Notre Dame High School* in Fairfield, Connecticut, who took pity on the freshman who couldn't tell a preposition from a participle (be it dangling or not); my co-workers at newspapers and later on at Ketchum Public Relations for playfully chiding me over my lack of grammatical prowess. I should also mention a co-worker at IBM, who once described the first draft of anything I wrote by saying, "Oh, yeah, his stuff is a hoot to edit." Negative feedback often equals positive motivation.

Besides my wife, Susan, to whom I dedicate this book, I also want to recognize and thank the positive influence from my sisters, Patricia and Geri, whose academic achievements made me want to improve my own; and from my daughter, Kelly, whose intelligence, grit, and determination for her own success is a positive influence on me. A shout-out goes to Kelly's husband, Jason, and their son, Henry (who is three years old as I write this). Papa wrote a book, Henry. It isn't *Brown bear, brown bear, what do you see?*, but we can't all write the classics.

I would be terribly remiss if I also did not thank the team from Beaufort Books: Megan Trank, Olivia Fish, Kristen

Coale, and Mary Bisbee-Beek. It was Mary who first encountered me whilst I was trolling my way through endless days at the University of Pennsylvania's Annenberg School for Communication, who kept in touch with me over the years and, thankfully, believed there may be a book inside me. Mary, I think you were right.

* Friends from my days at Central High School in Bridgeport, Connecticut who may not remember; yes, I went to Notre Dame High School for my freshman year only. Then the Diocese of Bridgeport raised the tuition to a point where my parents could no longer afford it. It was heigh-ho, heigh-ho, off to the public high school I go.

Endnotes

INTRODUCTION

1 Bernstein, Theodore M. *The Careful Writer*, Atheneum Press, 1975.

2 Goodwin, Doris Kearns. *Team of Rivals: The Political Genius of Abraham Lincoln*. Penguin Books, 2013.

3 "Jacques Barzun Quotes." *BrainyQuote*. Accessed April 30, 2021. https://www.brainyquote.com/quotes/jacques_barzun_118702.

4 Chapman, et. al., *Monty Python's Life of Brian*, Handmade Films, 1979.

5 Liuzza, R.M. *Beowulf: a New Verse Translation*. Broadview Press, 1999.

6 Waxman, Olivia B. "Lots of People Have Theories About Neil Armstrong's 'One Small Step for Man' Quote. Here's What We Really Know." *Time*, July 15, 2019.

7 McCulloch, Gretchen. *Because Internet Understanding the New Rules of Language*. Riverhead Books, 2019.

8 Canning, Iain, Emile Sherman, Gareth Unwin, and David Seidler. *The King's Speech*. United States: The Weinstein Company, 2010.

9 Noonan, Peggy. *What I Saw at the Revolution: A Political Life in the Reagan Era*. Random House, 1990.

10 Tréguer, Pascal. "How Thomas Jefferson Was Berated for Coining 'Belittle'." *word histories,* August 10, 2020. https://wordhistories.net/2018/03/25/belittle-thomas-jefferson/.

11 Reilly, Katie. "'Nevertheless She Persisted:' Women's History Month Theme." *Time. Time*, March 1, 2018. https://time.com/5175901/elizabeth-warren-nevertheless-she-persisted-meaning/.

12   Martin, Peter. *The Dictionary Wars: The American Fight Over the English Language*. Princeton University Press, 2019.

13   "Geno's Removes Controversial 'Please Speak English' Sign from Window." *6abc Philadelphia*. WPVI-TV, October 14, 2016. https://6abc.com/genos-cheesesteak-speak-english-controversial/1553791/.

14   Burns, Ken. *Country Music*, Florentine Films, 2019.

15   "A Quote by Otto Von Bismarck." *Goodreads*. Accessed May 5, 2021. https://www.goodreads.com/quotes/95610-god-has-a-special-providence-for-fools-drunkards-and-the.

16   Roddenberry, Gene. *Star Trek: The Original Series*, Paramount, NBC Television, 1966.

17   Roddenberry, Gene. *Star Trek: The Next Generation*, Paramount, 1987.

18   Fallis, Timothy. "Gramma Wamma."

19   Bochco, Steven, and Michael Kozoli. Whole. *Hill Street Blues*. NBC, 1981.

20   Stern, Howard. *Howard Stern Comes Again*. Simon & Schuster, 2019.

GRAMMA WAMMA

1   Mencken, *The American Language*, Coyote Canyon Press, 2012.

2   *Ibid.*

3   Fallis, Timothy. "Gramma Wamma."

4   Kelman, Brett. "Vanderbilt Can't Build Murfreesboro Hospital after Clash of Tennessee Health Care Giants." *The Tennessean. Nashville Tennessean*, August 30, 2020. https://www.tennessean.com/story/news/health/2020/08/30/vanderbilt-not-allowed-build-new-hospital-murfreesboro/5647274002/.

5   Spears, Joseph. "Belmont Announces New 45,000-Square-Foot Indoor Practice Facility." *The Tennessean. Nashville Tennessean*, January 22, 2020. https://www.tennessean.com/story/sports/college/2020/01/22/belmont-basketball-volleyball-indoor-practice-facility/4539282002/.

6   "Chomping at the Bit." Accessed April 30, 2021. https://www.urbandictionary.com/define.php?term=Chomping+at+the+bit.

TYPOS AND PROOFREADING

1   Turney, Michael. I don't care - PR, December 1, 2010. https://
    www.nku.edu/~turney/prclass/readings/3eras1x.html.

2   Klein, Christopher. "10 Words and Phrases Popularized by Presidents."
    History.com. A&E Television Networks, February 12, 2016. https://www.
    history.com/news/10-words-and-phrases-popularized-by-presidents.

3   Staff writers, *ABC News*, May 2018.

4   "Loose." *Merriam-Webster*. Accessed May 5, 2021. https://
    www.merriam-webster.com/dictionary/loose.

5   "Lose." *Merriam-Webster*. Accessed May 5, 2021. https://
    www.merriam-webster.com/dictionary/lose.

6   Giles, Sandie. *How to Proofread Your Own Writing: Tips and Techniques
    to Help You Produce an Error-Free Manuscript*. Sandie Giles, 2013.

7   Strunk, William Jr, and E. B. White. *The Elements
    of Style*. Boston: Allyn and Bacon, 1972.

PUNCTUATION

1   Truss, Lynne. *Eats, Shoots & Leaves: The Zero Tolerance
    Approach to Punctuation*, Gotham Books, 2003.

2   H.L. Mencken, *The American Language*, Coyote Canyon Press, 2012.

3   "Hey." *Merriam-Webster*. Accessed April 30, 2021. https://
    www.merriam-webster.com/dictionary/hey.

4   Beatles. *Hey Jude*, George Martin, Trident Studios, 31 July 1968.

5   Perlman, Merrill. "AP Hyphen Outrage Continues with Guidance
    Update." *Columbia Journalism Review*. Accessed May 5, 2021. https://
    www.cjr.org/language_corner/ap-hyphens-guidance-update.php.

6   Richards, John. The Apostrophe Protection Society. Accessed
    April 30, 2021. http://www.apostrophe.org.uk/.

7   "Apostrophe Campaign Ends Due to 'Ignorance and Laziness'."
     BBC News. BBC, November 29, 2019. https://www.bbc.
     com/news/uk-england-lincolnshire-50602665.

8   MCulloch, 47.

9   Staff., University of Chicago Press Editorial. *Chicago
     Manual of Style*. University of Chicago Press, 2017.

10   Twain, Mark. *The Autobiography of Mark Twain*,
     University of California Press, 2012.

11   Watson, Cecilia. *Semicolon: The Past, Present, and
     Future of a Misunderstood Mark*, CCCO, 2019.

12   Courtesy of Laura S. Trombley, Ph.D., Southwestern University.

WRITE WHAT YOU MEAN AND MEAN WHAT YOU WRITE

1   Episode. *F.R.I.E.N.D.S.* 1, no. 1. NBC, September 22, 1994.

2   Davis, Jim. *Garfield*, 19 June 1978.

3   Schulz, Charles M. *Charlie Brown*, 2 October 1950.

4   Breathed, Berkley. *Bloom County*, 9 December 1980.

5   Covey, Stephen R., Larry H. Freeman, and Breck England. *FranklinCovey
     Style Guide for Business and Technical Communication*. FT Press, 2012.

6   "'In the Man, or in the Jackass?'." *The Atlanta Journal-
     Constitution*, July 4, 2015. https://www.ajc.com/news/opinion/
     the-man-the-jackass/QL3lGrn2sTGxIhWKdPeMQK/.

7   Diorio, Joe. "Park Expects Damage." *The Hour*,
     Norwalk, Connecticut, January 1980.

8   Newell, Sean. "Headline: 'Amphibious' Pat Venditte Makes MLB
     Debut." *VICE*, June 9, 2015. https://www.vice.com/en/article/
     qkyzqv/headline-amphibious-pat-venditte-makes-mlb-debut.

9   Jones, Meghan. "11 Real (and Hilarious) Newspaper Typos You
     Won't Believe Were Printed." *Reader's Digest*, June 5, 2019.
     https://www.rd.com/article/hilarious-newspaper-typos/.

10 Allen, Kelly. "Kentucky Removed A Confederate Statue And An Old Bottle Of Bourbon Was Found Inside Of The Pedestal." *Delish*, September 15, 2020. https://www.delish.com/food-news/a32868428/kentucky-confederate-statue-bourbon/.

11 News of Fashion. "Cardi B on Raising Her Daughter, Bernie Sanders, and Coordinating Outfits with Offset: Vogue." News of Fashion, October 11, 2019. https://newsoffashion.com/cardi-b-on-raising-her-daughter-bernie-sanders-and-coordinating-outfits-with-offset-vogue/.

12 Stolberg, Sheryl Gay, and David Stout. "Elijah Cummings, Powerful Democrat Who Investigated Trump, Dies at 68." *The New York Times*, October 17, 2019. https://www.nytimes.com/2019/10/17/us/politics/elijah-cummings-death-illness.html.

13 Jaidka, Kokil, Alvin Zhou, and Yphtach Lelkes. "Brevity Is the Soul of Twitter: The Constraint Affordance and Political Discussion." *Journal of Communication* 69, no. 4 (2019): 345–72. https://doi.org/10.1093/joc/jqz023.

14 CNN, "Watch Donald Trump and Vladmir Putin's Full Press Conference," YouTube, July 2018.

15 "Contractions in Formal Writing: What's Allowed, What's Not." APA Style 6th Edition Blog. Accessed April 30, 2021. https://blog.apastyle.org/apastyle/2015/12/contractions-in-formal-writing-whats-allowed-whats-not.html#:~:text=Contractions%20are%20a%20part%20of,leave%20the%20contraction%20as%2Dis.

THE BUSINESS OF WRITING

1 "Cringeworthy." Merriam-Webster. Merriam-Webster. Accessed May 3, 2021. https://www.merriam-webster.com/dictionary/cringeworthy.

2 Eidenmuller, Michael E. American Rhetoric: Ronald Reagan -- First Inaugural Address. Delivered 20 January, 1981. Accessed May 3, 2021. https://www.americanrhetoric.com/speeches/ronaldreagandfirstinaugural.html.

3   Hansen, Lily. "Talking to Strangers is my Self Care," Filmed January 2020 in Nashville, Tennessee. TedXNashvilleWomen video, 18:36. https://www.ted. com/talks/lily_clayton_hansen_talking_to_strangers_is_my_self_care/up-next

4   Broadcast. *90th Academy Awards*. ABC, March 4, 2018.

5   "Sound Bite." *Merriam-Webster. Merriam-Webster.* Accessed May 5, 2021. https://www.merriam-webster.com/dictionary/sound%20bite.

6   "America Is Open for Business." National Archives and Records Administration. National Archives and Records Administration, January 20, 2012. https://obamawhitehouse. archives.gov/blog/2012/01/20/america-open-business.

7   "Greta Thunberg's World Economic Forum 2019 Special Address - Greta Thunberg." *Open Transcripts*, January 24, 2019. http://opentranscripts. org/transcript/greta-thunberg-world-economic-forum-2019/.

8   *Funny Girl.* United States: Rastar, 1968.

9   "Remarks of President John F. Kennedy at the Rudolph Wilde Platz, Berlin, June 26, 1963." Remarks of President John F. Kennedy at the Rudolph Wilde Platz, Berlin, June 26, 1963 | JFK Library. Accessed May 3, 2021. https://www.jfklibrary.org/archives/other-resources/john-f-kennedy-speeches/berlin-w-germany-rudolph-wilde-platz-19630626.

10   "That We Here Highly Resolve That These Dead Shall Not Have Died in Vain ... / Berryman." The Library of Congress. Accessed May 3, 2021. https://www.loc.gov/item/2016678408/.

11   *Dirty Harry.* United States: The Malpaso Company, 1971.

12   "Spike Lee Quotes." BrainyQuote. Xplore. Accessed May 3, 2021. https://www.brainyquote.com/quotes/spike_lee_263519.

13   "Text of Steve Jobs' Commencement Address (2005)." *Stanford News*, June 12, 2017. https://news.stanford.edu/2005/06/14/jobs-061505/.

14   Wills, Garry. *Lincoln at Gettysburg: The Words That Remade America.* New York: Simon & Schuster Paperbacks, 2007.

15 *Star Trek II: The Wrath of Khan*. United States: Paramount Pictures, 1982.

16 "Inaugural Addresses of the Presidents of the United States: from George Washington 1789 to George Bush 1989." Avalon Project - Documents in Law, History and Diplomacy. Accessed May 3, 2021. https://avalon.law.yale.edu/20th_century/clinton1.asp.

17 Holden, Michael. "'We'll Meet Again': Queen Elizabeth Invokes WW2 Spirit to Defeat Coronavirus." *Reuters*. Thomson Reuters, April 5, 2020. https://www.reuters.com/article/us-health-coronavirus-britain-queen/well-meet-again-queen-elizabeth-invokes-ww2-spirit-to-defeat-coronavirus-idUSKBN21N0TQ.

18 Ruane, Michael. "'The Boys of Pointe Du Hoc': The Reagan D-Day Speech That Moved a Nation." *The Washington Post*. WP Company, June 5, 2019. https://www.washingtonpost.com/history/2019/06/05/boys-pointe-du-hoc-reagan-d-day-speech-that-moved-nation/.

19 "Their Finest Hour." International Churchill Society, January 14, 2018. https://winstonchurchill.org/resources/speeches/1940-the-finest-hour/their-finest-hour/.

20 Public Affairs, UC Berkeley| May 16, and Public Affairs. "Sheryl Sandberg, Facebook Chief, Speaks from the Heart at Commencement 2016." *Berkeley News*, May 17, 2016. https://news.berkeley.edu/2016/05/16/sheryl-sandberg-2016-commencement-address/.

21 "'It's Evolution, Man. Eventually the Student Becomes the Teacher.'." Big Sean Quote. Accessed May 3, 2021. https://quotefancy.com/quote/1406713/Big-Sean-It-s-evolution-man-Eventually-the-student-becomes-the-teacher.

22 "Text of Steve Jobs' Commencement Address (2005)." *Stanford News*, June 12, 2017. https://news.stanford.edu/2005/06/14/jobs-061505/.

23 Alter, Alexandra. "Amanda Gorman Captures the Moment, in Verse." *The New York Times*. The New York Times, January 19, 2021. https://www.nytimes.com/2021/01/19/books/amanda-gorman-inauguration-hill-we-climb.html.

24   A Spotlight on a Primary Source by John F. Kennedy. "The Gilder
     Lehrman Institute of American History." John F. Kennedy's Inaugural
     Address, 1961 | Gilder Lehrman Institute of American History. Accessed
     May 3, 2021. https://www.gilderlehrman.org/history-resources/spotlight-
     primary-source/john-f-kennedy%E2%80%99s-inaugural-address-1961.

25   "Luckiest Man." Baseball Hall of Fame. Accessed May 3, 2021.
     https://baseballhall.org/discover-more/stories/baseball-history/
     lou-gehrig-luckiest-man#:~:text=It%20was%20on%20July%20
     4,the%20face%20of%20the%20earth.%E2%80%9D.

26   Carr, Nicholas. "Is Google Making Us Stupid?" *The Atlantic*. Atlantic
     Media Company, January 23, 2020. https://www.theatlantic.com/
     magazine/archive/2008/07/is-google-making-us-stupid/306868/.

27   DeMers, Jayson. "Is Bad Grammar Killing Your Brand?" *Forbes*.
     Forbes Magazine, July 21, 2014. https://www.forbes.com/sites/
     jaysondemers/2014/07/15/is-bad-grammar-killing-your-brand/.

28   Strunk, William Jr, and E. B. White. *The Elements
     of Style*. Boston: Allyn and Bacon, 1972.

29   Strunk, William Jr, and E. B. White, 86.

30   Staff., University of Chicago Press Editorial. *Chicago
     Manual of Style*. University of Chicago Press, 2017.

PHRASEOLOGY FOLLIES

1   "Rigged." *Merriam-Webster*. Accessed May 3, 2021. https://
     www.merriam-webster.com/dictionary/rigged.

2   "Rigged." *Urban Dictionary*. Accessed May 4, 2021. https://
     www.urbandictionary.com/define.php?term=rigged.

3   Simpson, J. A., and Michael Proffitt. "On Time." In *Oxford
     English Dictionary*. Oxford (England): Clarendon Press, 1997.

4   Blinder, Alan. "Was That Ralph Northam in Blackface? An
     Inquiry Ends Without Answers." *The New York Times*. The
     New York Times, May 22, 2019. https://www.nytimes.
     com/2019/05/22/us/ralph-northam-blackface-photo.html.

5   Allison, Natalie. "Gov. Bill Lee Pictured in Auburn Yearbook Wearing
     Confederate Army Uniform." *The Tennessean*. The Tennessean, February 21,
     2019. https://www.tennessean.com/story/news/politics/2019/02/21/bill-lee-
     tennessee-governor-auburn-yearbook-confederate-yearbook/2939636002/.

6   Gathright, Jenny. "Despite His Own Blackface Scandal, Virginia
     AG Says Governor Has Lost Public Trust." *NPR*. NPR, March 4,
     2019. https://www.npr.org/2019/03/04/700084752/despite-his-own-
     blackface-scandal-virginia-ag-says-governor-has-lost-public-trus.

7   "Rabbit Hole." *Merriam-Webster*. Accessed May 4, 2021. https://
     www.merriam-webster.com/dictionary/rabbit%20hole.

8   Bryan DeArdo Nov 15. "Myles Garrett Issues Apology after Striking
     Mason Rudolph with His Own Helmet." *CBSSports.com*, November
     15, 2019. https://www.cbssports.com/nfl/news/myles-garrett-issues-
     apology-after-striking-mason-rudolph-with-his-own-helmet/.

9   Cochrane, Emily, and Jennifer Medina. "End of Government Shutdown
     May Depend on the Definition of 'Wall'." *The New York Times*.
     The New York Times, December 27, 2018. https://www.nytimes.
     com/2018/12/26/us/politics/government-shutdown-wall.html.

10   "Wall." *Merriam-Webster*. Accessed May 4, 2021. https://
     www.merriam-webster.com/dictionary/wall.

11   "450 Years Later, We Are Still Speaking Shakespeare's Lines:
     MTM LinguaSoft." MTM LinguaSoft | Professional Language
     Translation Services, February 12, 2020. https://www.mtmlinguasoft.
     com/450-years-later-we-are-still-speaking-shakespeares-lines/.

12   "Allision." *Merriam-Webster*. Accessed May 4, 2021. https://
     www.merriam-webster.com/dictionary/allision.

13 "Francesco Maria Grimaldi - Scientist of the Day." Linda Hall Library, April 2, 2019. https://www.lindahall.org/francesco-maria-grimaldi/#:~:text=The%20maria%20(seas)%20 were%20named,%E2%80%93%20the%20Sea%20of%20 Cold).&text=By%20the%20time%20Riccioli%20got,R-enaissance%20and%2017th%20century%20scientists.

14 "Sea." *Merriam-Webster.* Accessed May 4, 2021. https://www.merriam-webster.com/dictionary/sea.

15 "Biosignature." *Merriam-Webster.* Accessed May 4, 2021. https://www.merriam-webster.com/dictionary/biosignature.

A FEW WORDS ABOUT NUMBERS

1 Staff., University of Chicago Press Editorial. *Chicago Manual of Style.* University of Chicago Press, 2017.

2 *ABC News.* ABC News Network. Accessed May 4, 2021. https://abcnews.go.com/GMA/video/high-tech-drones-steal-show-winter-olympics-52983788.

3 "Few." *Merriam-Webster.* Accessed May 4, 2021. https://www.merriam-webster.com/dictionary/few.

SWEAR IT OUT

1 Tharoor, Ishaan. "The F-Word Is Even Older than You Think." *The Washington Post.* WP Company, May 2, 2019. https://www.washingtonpost.com/news/worldviews/wp/2015/09/15/the-f-word-is-even-older-than-you-think/.

2 Mencken, H. L. *The American Language: an Inquiry into the Development of English in the United States.* West Valley City, UT: Waking Lion Press/The Editorium, LLC, 1921.

3 *Star Trek IV, the Voyage Home.* Hollywood, CA: Paramount Pictures, 1986.

4 "My Girl Trivia." IMDb. IMDb.com. Accessed May 4, 2021. https://www.imdb.com/title/tt0102492/trivia.

5   Bouton, Jim, and Neil Offen. *"I Managed Good, but Boy Did They Play Bad.".* New York: Dell Pub. Co., 1974.

6   "Joe Biden: 'This Is a Big Fucking Deal' | Richard Adams." *The Guardian.* Guardian News and Media, March 23, 2010. https://www.theguardian.com/world/richard-adams-blog/2010/mar/23/joe-biden-obama-big-fucking-deal-overheard.

7   Montopoli, Brian. "Levin Repeatedly References 'Sh**Ty Deal' at Goldman Hearing." *CBS News.* CBS Interactive, April 27, 2010. https://www.cbsnews.com/news/levin-repeatedly-references-shty-deal-at-goldman-hearing/.

8   Grant, Holly Butcher. "That 'Clusterf-k' Headline: How UNC's Newspaper Responded to a COVID 'Cluster' on Campus." *Journalism Institute,* August 19, 2020. https://www.pressclubinstitute.org/2020/08/17/that-clusterf-k-headline-how-uncs-newspaper-responded-to-a-covid-cluster-on-campus/.

9   "Clusterfuck." *Merriam-Webster.* Accessed May 4, 2021. https://www.merriam-webster.com/dictionary/clusterfuck.

10 McCluskey, Michael. "Profanity and the President: News Use of Trump's Shithole Comment - Michael McCluskey, 2019." *SAGE Journals.* Accessed May 4, 2021. https://journals.sagepub.com/doi/abs/10.1177/0739532919855782.

11 Schake, Kori. "Presidents Get the Military Leaders They Deserve." *Foreign Policy.* Foreign Policy, May 11, 2015. https://foreignpolicy.com/2015/05/11/presidents-get-the-military-leaders-they-deserve/.

12 Shoop, Tom. "Air Force Official JFK Called 'Silly Bastard' Immortalized on Film." *Government Executive.* Government Executive, April 10, 2021. https://www.govexec.com/federal-news/2014/03/air-force-official-jfk-called-silly-bastard-immortalized-film/80317/.

13 Haber, Matt. "Daily Show's LBJ 'Piss' Take." *Observer.* Observer, November 19, 2008. https://observer.com/2008/11/idaily-showis-lbj-piss-take/.

14 Ryan Schocket. "19 Times Taylor Swift Cursed." *BuzzFeed.* BuzzFeed, February 1, 2017. https://www.buzzfeed.com/ryanschocket2/tiger-plus-lion-equals-whore.

15   Allen, Barbara. "'That Was the First Headline Idea That We Had': The Origin Story of The Onion's Most Hilarious Cover." *Poynter*, July 19, 2019. https://www.poynter.org/reporting-editing/2019/that-was-the-first-headline-idea-that-we-had-the-origin-story-of-the-onions-most-hilarious-cover/.

16   Flood, Brian. "New York Post's Front Page Headline about Jeff Bezos' Nude Selfie Scandal Gets Online Applause." *Fox News*. FOX News Network, February 9, 2019. https://www.foxnews.com/entertainment/new-york-post-jeff-bezos-headline-nude-selfie-scandal-online-applause.

17   Dicker, Rachel. "Daily News Runs Cover of Trump As Angry Judge: 'We Are F*#%'D'." *Mediaite*, June 28, 2018. https://www.mediaite.com/online/daily-news-runs-cover-of-trump-as-angry-judge-we-are-fd/.

18   Favilla, Emmy. "BuzzFeed Style Guide." *BuzzFeed*. *BuzzFeed*, April 27, 2021. https://www.buzzfeed.com/emmyf/buzzfeed-style-guide.

19   Spj. "SPJ Code of Ethics - Society of Professional Journalists." Society of Professional Journalists - Improving and protecting journalism since 1909. Accessed May 4, 2021. https://www.spj.org/ethicscode.asp.

DON'T LABEL "DIS" LANGUAGE

1   "Dis." *Merriam-Webster*. Accessed May 4, 2021. https://www.merriam-webster.com/dictionary/dis.

2   Sornig, Karl. *Lexical Innovation: A Study of Slang, Colloquialisms and Casual Speech*. Amsterdam: J. Benjamins, 1985.

3   Swenson, Kyle. "Who Came up with the Term 'Sexual Harassment'?" *The Washington Post*. WP Company, April 29, 2019. https://www.washingtonpost.com/news/morning-mix/wp/2017/11/22/who-came-up-with-the-term-sexual-harassment/.

4   Inskeep, Steve. "Shooting Victims Face Lifelong Disabilities, Financial Burdens, Newspaper Finds." *NPR*, December 11, 2018. https://www.npr.org/2018/12/11/675505101/shooting-victims-face-lifelong-disabilities-financial-burdens-newspaper-finds.

5   "'Baby Joe' Clyde Daniels Case: WKRN News." *WKRN News 2*. Accessed May 4, 2021. https://www.wkrn.com/baby-joe/.

6   Jamieson, Kathleen H., Albarracin, Dolores (2020). The Relation between Media Consumption and Misinformation at the Outset of the SARS-CoV-2 Pandemic in the US, *The Harvard Kennedy School (HKS) Misinformation Review*, Volume 1, Issue 2

7   Armus, Teo. "'Really Not a Great Look': Chris Cuomo Apologizes for Pronoun Gaffe at LGBTQ Candidate Town Hall." *The Washington Post.* WP Company, October 11, 2019. https://www.washingtonpost. com/nation/2019/10/11/chris-cuomo-pronoun-gaffe-lgbt-forum/.

8   Press, Associated. "Coronavirus Keeps Spreading, Trump Says 'Toughest' Weeks Coming." *Chicago Sun-Times*, April 4, 2020. https://chicago.suntimes.com/coronavirus/2020/4/4/21208313/ coronavirus-trump-covid-19-toughest-weeks-coming.

9   "Social Distancing." *Merriam-Webster.* Accessed May 4, 2021. https:// www.merriam-webster.com/dictionary/social%20distancing.

10   "Asymptomatic." *Merriam-Webster.* Accessed May 4, 2021. https:// www.merriam-webster.com/dictionary/asymptomatic.

11   "Covidiot." *Urban Dictionary.* Accessed May 4, 2021. https:// www.urbandictionary.com/define.php?term=Covidiot.

12   "House Arrest." *Merriam-Webster.* Accessed May 5, 2021. https:// www.merriam-webster.com/dictionary/house%20arrest.

13   Horn, Austin. "'Please Scream Inside Your Heart,' Japanese Amusement Park Tells Thrill-Seekers." *NPR.* NPR, July 9, 2020. https://www.npr. org/sections/coronavirus-live-updates/2020/07/09/889394605/please- scream-inside-your-heart-japanese-amusement-park-tells-thrill-seekers.

14   "'La Covid': Coronavirus Acronym Is Feminine, Académie Française Says." *The Guardian.* Guardian News and Media, May 13, 2020. https://www.theguardian.com/world/2020/may/13/le-la-covid- coronavirus-acronym-feminine-academie-francaise-france.

15 Martel, Jay. "Lexicon for a Pandemic." *The New Yorker*. July 20, 2020, n.d.

16 "Israeli Study Says Using Emojis in Work Emails Conveys Incompetence." *Algemeiner.com*. Accessed May 4, 2021. https://www.algemeiner.com/2017/08/18/israeli-study-says-using-emojis-in-work-emails-conveys-incompetence/.

17 Wagner, James. "Who Needs Trade Talks? These Days, General Managers Just Use Emojis." *The New York Times*. The New York Times, January 4, 2018. https://www.nytimes.com/2018/01/04/sports/baseball/general-managers-texting.html.

18 Fane, Jennifer. (2016). Exploring the use of emoji as a visual research method for eliciting young children's voices in childhood research. Early Child Development and Care. 188. 10.1080/03004430.2016.1219730.

19 Dishman, Lydia. "The Business Etiquette Guide To Emojis." *Fast Company*. Fast Company, July 15, 2016. https://www.fastcompany.com/3061807/the-business-etiquette-guide-to-emojis.

20 Acho, Emmanuel. *Uncomfortable Conversations with a Black Man*, n.d. https://uncomfortableconvos.com/.

21 Andrews EE, Forber-Pratt AJ, Mona LR, Lund EM, Pilarski CR, Balter R. #SaytheWord: A disability culture commentary on the erasure of "disability". Rehabil Psychol. 2019 May;64(2):111-118. doi: 10.1037/rep0000258. Epub 2019 Feb 14. PMID: 30762412.

FESTIVUS, COLLECTION OF GRAMMATICAL PET PEEVES

1 Whole. *Seinfeld* 9, no. 10. NBC, December 18, 1997.

2 Bromwich, Jonah Engel. "Bulletin! The 'Internet' Is About to Get Smaller." *The New York Times*. The New York Times, May 24, 2016. https://www.nytimes.com/2016/05/25/business/media/internet-to-be-lowercase-in-new-york-times-and-associated-press.html?smid=tw-nytimes&smtyp=cur.

3 D'Orazio, Dante. "The Associated Press Style Guide Will No Longer Capitalize 'Internet'." *The Verge*. The Verge, April 2, 2016. https://www.theverge.com/2016/4/2/11352744/ap-style-guide-will-no-longer-capitalize-internet.

4   "They." *Merriam-Webster*. Accessed May 4, 2021. https://
     www.merriam-webster.com/dictionary/they.

5   "Reax." *Urban Dictionary*. Accessed May 4, 2021. https://
     www.urbandictionary.com/define.php?term=Reax.

6   Reston, Maeve. Donald Trump's legal defeats pile up while
     his attacks on Georgia's election system raise GOP concerns.
     Accessed May 4, 2021. https://www.msn.com/en-us/news/
     politics/donald-trumps-legal-defeats-pile-up-while-his-attacks-on-
     georgias-election-system-raise-gop-concerns/ar-BB1br2kq.

7   *Elf*. Film. United States: New Line Cinema, 2003.

8   *Santa Clause*. Film. United States: Buena Vista Pictures, 1994.

9   Society for the Confluence of Festivals in India. "Santa Names
     Around the World." Christmas Day. Accessed May 4, 2021.
     https://www.christmas-day.org/multiculturism-santas.html.

10   *Die Hard*. Film. United States: Twentieth Century Fox, 1988.

11   Tung, Angela. "A Brief History of Yippee-Ki-Yay." *The Week - All you
     need to know about everything that matters*. The Week, July 18, 2013.
     https://theweek.com/articles/462065/brief-history-yippeekiyay.

12   "What Is a Reindeer?" *Macmillan Dictionary Blog*, December 15, 2017.
     https://www.macmillandictionaryblog.com/reindeer#:~:text=Origin%20
     of%20the%20word,animal%20commonly%20known%20as%20reindeer.

13   "Bauble." *Merriam-Webster*. Accessed May 5, 2021. https://
     www.merriam-webster.com/dictionary/bauble.

14   Andrews, Evan. "Why Do We Kiss Under the Mistletoe?" *History.
     com*. A&E Television Networks, December 24, 2013. https://
     www.history.com/news/why-do-we-kiss-under-the-mistletoe.

15   "FRANKINCENSE: Overview, Uses, Side Effects, Precautions, Interactions,
     Dosing and Reviews." *WebMD*. WebMD. Accessed May 5, 2021. https://
     www.webmd.com/vitamins/ai/ingredientmono-448/frankincense.

16   "MYRRH: Overview, Uses, Side Effects, Precautions, Interactions, Dosing and Reviews." WebMD. *WebMD.* Accessed May 5, 2021. https://www.webmd.com/vitamins/ai/ingredientmono-570/myrrh.

17   Communications, Vanderbilt Division of. "Fact or Fake? The Role of Knowledge Neglect in Misinformation." Vanderbilt University. Vanderbilt University, May 15, 1970. https://news.vanderbilt.edu/2020/05/15/fact-or-fake-the-role-of-knowledge-neglect-in-misinformation/.

THE FINAL WORD

1   Siegel, E. "The Color of Space." *ScienceBlogs,* September 14, 2011. https://scienceblogs.com/startswithabang/2011/09/14/the-color-of-space.

2   Musante, Fred. "Teachers' Strike Stirs Bitter Memories." *The New York Times.* The New York Times, February 1, 1998. https://www.nytimes.com/1998/02/01/nyregion/teachers-strike-stirs-bitter-memories.html.

3   Walker, Mort. *Beetle Bailey,* 4 September 1950.

A NOTE FROM THE AUTHOR

1   Zinsser, William. *On Writing Well.* Harper Paperbacks, 2013.

2   Swartzwelder, John. Episode. *The Simpsons* 8, no. 18. Fox, March 16, 1997.